BEER HACKS

100 TIPS, TRICKS, AND PROJECTS

★ BEN ROBINSON ★

Workman Publishing • New York

Library of Congress Cataloging-in-Publication Data is available.

ISBN 978-1-5235-0110-6

Interior design by Jean-Marc Troadec
Cover art: Beer background: Yuji Kotani/Stockbyte/Getty Images
Back cover and interior illustrations © by Lee Woodgate/Son of Alan

Workman books are available at special discounts when purchased in bulk for premiums and sales promotions as well as for fund-raising or educational use. Special editions or book excerpts can also be created to specification. For details, contact the Special Sales Director at the address below, or send an email to specialmarkets@workman.com.

Workman Publishing Co., Inc.
225 Varick Street
New York, NY 10014-4381
workman.com

WORKMAN is a registered trademark of Workman Publishing Co., Inc.

Printed in China
First printing August 2018

10 9 8 7 6 5 4 3 2 1

NOTICE TO READERS: While following along with the beer hacks in this book should be a fun and rewarding experience, you should always take care and use caution and sound judgment. The publisher and author of this book do not and cannot assume any responsibility for property damage or bodily injury caused to you or others as a result of any misinterpretation or misapplication of the information or instructions provided in this book.

To my astounding and unnecessarily understanding wife, Rebecca,
who allowed me to shoot cans of beer with a fire extinguisher,
in our home, for research, and my daughter, Lyle, who isn't allowed
to read this book until she's twenty-one.

Contents

Introduction

Ben Robinson

"Oh, cool! But . . . what's a beer hack?" That's the response you get from literally any person upon telling them you're writing a book called *Beer Hacks*.

So. What *is* a beer hack? The definition's pretty darn flexible, which is part of the fun.

There are ways to optimize or add to its flavor, to store it so that it tastes the way you deserve, to make it deliciously cold within minutes, and to keep it cold when you can't find a fridge or don't live on Hoth. You can craft amazing things out of bottles and cans, often by lighting other things on fire. You can cook with it and employ it to make cocktails to ride shotgun with your meal. There are also what I call "beer life hacks," which range from involving beer more intimately in your shower routine to figuring out what to do with your beer stash in the event of nuclear annihilation, after which we'll probably all want a drink.

The landscape of beer is nearly endless, offering a multiverse of breweries, styles, and reasons to crack one open. It's also highly personal—choosing a beer is one

hundred percent about what YOU want, right now. Some of these hacks are largely universal (say, the making-them-cold-quickly stuff), while others are for the drinkers who are ready to go a little deeper than they ever thought. Much like beers themselves, not every hack is for everyone, but some are definitely, definitely for you. Find those, use them, and maybe even play around with your favorites to take things another level further. The most crucial thing to remember is: Have some damn fun. If you haven't, I (and beer itself) have failed.

Beer is beautiful. It's also capable of far more than most people realize. This book is here to hold your hand (the one not already clutching a beer) and guide you through these hack-y worlds. So read up, drink up, and most important, be careful with all that fire.

Beer Terms

to Hack Your Way to Sounding Cooler and More Informed

Like any good subculture, beer lovers have created their own language, complete with words for things they prize, things they despise, and things called "beached whales." A complete glossary of beer-related terms would be an entirely different book, but here are a handful of the most fun and evocative to get you going. There will not be a quiz! But I'll refer back to some of them throughout the rest of the book, so actually, there will kind of be a quiz.

01 **CRUSHABLE:** A beer you can drink quickly, or, crush. This is generally used for lower-ABV (or, alcohol by volume) beers that are designed to go down easy (between 4% and 6% or so), but it can also reference, say, a double IPA (which generally comes in around 8% and up) that has a unique mix of punch and smoothness. Those generally get the modifier of "dangerously" crushable. It is a very correct modifier.

02 **SHELF TURD:** A beer that's been sitting in a store, getting more cobwebby and sadder by the day, as it pushes past its drinking prime. Most of these are beers that (for whatever silly reason) beer-selling establishments buy en masse, and then nobody wants, eventually leading to their turd-ness.

03 **WHALE:** That particular beer you oh so desperately want but can't ever seem to get your hands on. Maybe it's a limited release, maybe you live on the opposite side of the country or world from where it's available, but . . . you just can't get it. Yes, this is a Moby Dick thing.

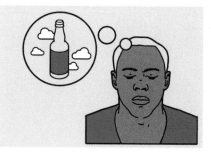

04 **_DRAIN POUR:_** A beer that's so skunked, spoiled, off, or just plain bad that there's only one thing to do with it—pour it right down the drain. Even with the cheeky name to soften the blow, this is always a sad moment.

05 **_BOMBER:_** The big, generally 22-ounce bottles that beer is sometimes packaged in, most especially strong, barrel-aged examples that really live up to the name

06 **_BEACHED WHALE:_** People are most likely to spot a beached whale the morning after a long night of enjoying wonderful beers, when they head to the fridge to make the hash browns they so desperately need and find an amazing bottle (generally a large bomber) sitting in the fridge, horrifically half-finished. Even worse is when it's on the table and warm beyond repair, in addition to just flat.

07 *LIGHTSTRUCK:* A cool, AC/DC-ish way of saying "skunked." Both terms mean that evil, evil light has murdered your beer's taste, and it now seems like Pepé Le Pew has sprayed something not nice into your beer.

08 *BUGS:* Wild yeast and/or bacteria that's used in fermentation to create sour beers, wild ales, and other such funky styles.

How to
Make Your Beers Cold—Quick

Every beer drinker has been in the Worst of All Situations: coming home after a long, hard day at the quarry and realizing that (1) you really need to get a cushier job, and worse, (2) the fridge is empty and all the beer in the house is every bit as warm as the freshly used multiblade gang saw from back down at the quarry.

This generally leaves two options: drinking that beer warm, or drinking zero beer at all. So, actually, one option. But luckily for warm-beer-havers everywhere, there are a raft of truly innovative night-saving means by which to get your beer ice-cold in just minutes—or even less time, depending on what you've got available.

09 THE *WET RAG* + THE *FREEZER* METHOD

Let's start with the lowest-effort approach of the four.

COLD BEER ETA: 7 TO 10 MINUTES

Grab your least-gross rag, get it good and wet with cold water, then wring out the excess. The idea is that you want the water to freeze around the beer as quickly as possible. So, if it's oversaturated, that's going to be tough. Paper towels can work if you're in a ragless pinch, but really, a rag or dish towel or even an actual towel is what you want here.

Once it's prepped, grab your beer and wrap it up, going once around the can or bottle with the rag/towel, or a few spins with the paper towels. Then just toss the beer in the freezer (if you can rest it on a tray or bag of ice, all the better), close the door (crucial step!), and set your stopwatch for 7 minutes (although if your freezer is crammed, it may take 10). A standard 12-ounce can or bottle may not even take that long, and that time parameter should get a 22-ounce bomber decently chilled as well.

When the time's up, your towel should be frozen somewhat solid and want desperately to stay attached to the bottle. But you, beer-deprived as you may be, will be able to summon the strength to rip it off and reveal a wonderful beer chilled to appropriate enjoyment temperatures.

Be sure to wrap it snugly to show you care.

One big word of warning: No matter the circumstances, do NOT leave your beer in the freezer for longer than 20 minutes or so. For one, it will freeze like so many Otter Pops before it, and for two, it's impossible to drink beers through freezer doors.

Forgetting it's in there: Don't do that.

10 THE *SPIN IT IN A BUCKET FULL OF ICE + SALT* METHOD

Yes, your hand is going to get cold with this one.

COLD BEER ETA: 3 MINUTES

All you need for this is water; a bowl, bucket, beer pitcher, or other fairly large receptacle to put that water in; enough salt to make all the slugs in your neighborhood uncomfortable; and a hand that likes to spin things/doesn't mind getting a little cold. (Note: This is great for hotels, which often don't have a fridge but do have all the rest of these things, especially if you're bold enough to ask for a hundred salt packets from room service.)

If you remember ninth-grade chemistry class, you'll remember that protons have a positive charge, electrons have a negative one, and the emergency eye wash is completely hilarious to trick people into drinking water out of. You may or may not also recall the principles behind boiling point elevation/freezing point depression.

The technical definition involves entropy and thermodynamics, sooo . . . let's skip all that and say: If you put salt into water, it makes the temperature at which the water freezes go way down. So, if you put salt into water and ice, it causes the ice to melt, making the whole bath significantly colder than ice plus water minus salt. Which makes your beer cold, if you put it in. It's the same exact set of principles that make antifreeze work, but since you'll be drinking the beer, maybe don't think about that.

There are a couple of key moves to keep in mind here. First, you're not using a pinch of salt; you need a lot. Like, cups of the stuff. Literal cups! Just dump it in and stir, then add as much ice as you can find.

Make sure you don't add so much that the water spills over when you put the beer in.

Salt it like you would a T-bone, after a highly positive physical.

Yes, your hand will get cold.

The next is that once it goes into the bath, you need to spin the bottle or can round and round as much as possible, which will accelerate the cooling process and make your hand remarkably cold (you will be a much happier/less frostbitten beer drinker if you do this with a bottle instead of a can, so you can grab and spin the neck outside the ice bath). But that just means it's working, right? Three minutes of spinning should get your beer exactly where you want it.

11 THE *FIRE EXTINGUISHER* METHOD

It may not be the most cost-efficient approach, but blasting your beer with a fire extinguisher will certainly get it good and cold. **COLD BEER ETA: 20 TO 30 SECONDS**

The most important thing: You need a carbon dioxide extinguisher, not a monoammonium phosphate version. It works by starving a fire of oxygen, but that same overabundance of CO_2 also makes things very, very chilly. This hack is dead simple. You just put the beer in a bucket so it stays in one place (also, holding it would likely prove to be unwise), trigger the fire extinguisher in quick, repeating 1- to-2-second blasts at the beer, quickly rinse it off, and drink. Twenty to 30 seconds should do it, depending on the size of the beer. All CO_2 extinguishers have a "horn" from which the discharge emits, but some have one that's large enough to rest a beer snugly inside. If yours does, definitely do that, as the gas will contact the beer more directly and speed up the cooling process. Also . . . do this outside. You'll see why.

Just remember to recharge the fire

Let the bucket, not your hand, hold the beer.

You PROBABLY won't die either way, but just to be safe. . . .

extinguisher, in case there's an actual fire, and to put your beers in the fridge more promptly in the future, so you don't have to keep recharging fire extinguishers.

Important note: Fire extinguishers are simple to use correctly and safely, but if you're not doing that, they can be pretty damn dangerous. The main rules are: (1) Don't discharge the extinguisher toward your body or anyone else's; (2) Be sure you're using it in a highly ventilated area (like outside, as recommended!); and (3) Never, ever look into the horn, even if you're not using it.

12 THE *COMPRESSED AIR* METHOD

Forget unrooting bagel remains from your laptop—this office supply closet staple can *really* prove its worth by ensuring your beer is appropriately chilled. If you don't have spare fire extinguishers sitting around, there's still hope for a remarkably quick cold-beer turnaround.

COLD BEER ETA: 1 MINUTE TO 1 MINUTE, 30 SECONDS

If you turn the compressed air can upside down and pull the trigger, it'll expel liquid instead of gas—ice-cold liquid. But you can't just spray and pray; the trick is to get your beer and the canister's contents in as close quarters as possible.

A strong move here is to take a good, firm plastic food storage container (the smaller the better, but it obviously has to fit the beer) and drill a hole just slightly larger than the compressed air can's stem in the side. Toss the beer in, slap the top on, and duct tape down the lid so it doesn't go flying when you fire. Then, turn that can upside down, insert the stem, and let 'er rip. You may need to use two canisters, as they exhaust themselves fairly quickly. And just to be safe, you'll

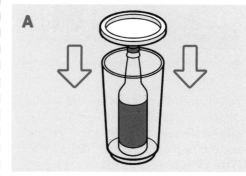

A

Make sure the bottle fits with the top on before you drill anything.

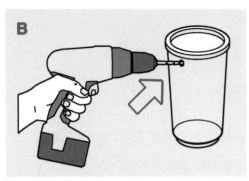

Avoid using the fancy plastic food storage container you got for your wedding.

Position the can upside down and fire!

Make sure the tape seal goes all the way around the top.

WIPE

Cleanliness has never been more important.

probably want to wear gloves—this stuff is colder than the glare you'll get from the Facilities Manager when they find out you've been robbing them blind and NOT EVEN GIVING THEM ANY BEER.

The only thing to worry about here is that some compressed air cans contain a bittering agent that makes the air taste terrible (no matter how much you enjoy hoppy beer) so that kids who stumble across an air can don't get any bad ideas about inhaling it, which is not advisable. Which means you should wipe down your now Hoth-cold beer, and probably also pour it into a glass.

How to
Keep Your Beers Cold When You Don't Have a Fridge/Cooler (But You Do Have Ice)

This is a common problem, but never fear—we've got two very easy solutions.

13 THE *ICE IN THE CASE* MOVE

Perhaps the most intelligent example of cardboard reuse in history

The list of what you'll need here is brief: a twelve-pack of bottled beer with the box intact, a plastic garbage bag, and ice.

First, yank out all the beer and also (if they're in there) those little cardboard divider thingies that keep your beers from crashing into each other inside the case. Then layer the garbage bag inside the case and replace those little cardboard divider thingies that keep your beers from crashing into each other.

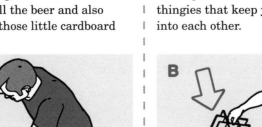

A

Bag → box

B

Divider thingies → bag

Now put your beers back in, then dump as much of the ice as will possibly fit, and voilà: You just made a fridge, a limited mess, and a reeeeeeeeal impact on your afternoon.

Ice → beer

14 THE *ICE BAG IS YOUR COOLER* MOVE

Sure, the floor may get a little wet, but cold beers are far more important.

Another pretty simple one here: You literally just tear a small hole in a medium-to-large bag of ice from the store, then work your beers deeper and deeper into the ice until you have a bag of ice that looks like it should be on someone's shoulder in the crazy-fan section at a Raiders game. You should be able to squeeze at least a six-pack in, maybe more.

A

Just jam it right into that ice bag.

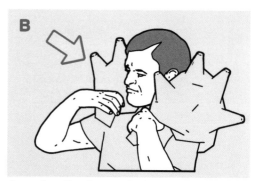

B

A very functional way to look insane

Ingenious Methods

for Opening Beers When You Don't Have a Bottle Opener

Your beer is now good and cold, which is a fantastic step. But—whoops!—you recently dropped and shattered your novelty bottle opener that looked like a lucha libre wrestler putting the neck of the beer in a headlock. Luckily, throughout the centuries, many an ingenious soul has used a tidy combination of simple physics and raw desperation to discover a myriad of ways to access their beer.

METHOD 1:

15 UM, JUST *DRINK BEER OUT OF A CAN*

I know this sounds crazy, but . . .

Right. Riiiiight. And so many fantastic breweries exclusively sheathe their wares in silver these days. But bottles are not going away, which means this can't be your lone solution.

Genius comes in simple forms sometimes.

METHOD 2:

16 THE *LIGHTER* MOVE

Perhaps the most essential beer-opening hack in history.

Do you remember when you learned about simple machines such as inclined planes and wedges in grade school? Of course not. Good thing you bought this book! The simple machine you're going to be using in this instance is a lever. That lever will be a lighter, a device that extensive scientific research I did in a bar last Saturday night proves will be available in ninety-five percent of all beer-drinking situations.

WHAT YOU'LL NEED: One bottle of beer, one lighter (preferably a Bic—they can take the most abuse)

STEP 1: Grab your beer bottle by the neck, wrapping your pinky, ring, and middle fingers around it *as tightly as you* *can*—none of the following advice will be worthwhile if you drop the bottle while everything else is going on. Keep your index finger semiextended about half an inch away from the neck, and line up its tip with the bottom of the cap.

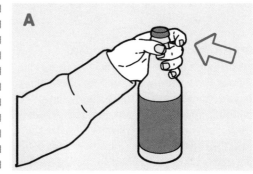

The initial grip is crucial.

STEP 2: With your other hand, wedge the non-fire-producing end of the lighter under the cap, and lock it in between the two joints in the middle of your index finger on the hand that's wrapping the neck. Your index finger has just become your fulcrum, another word from Simple Machines Class you don't remember.

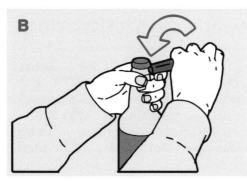

Make sure the end of the lighter gets wedged tightly under the cap's edge.

STEP 3: Now you must execute two coordinated moves at once: (1) pushing the lighter downward with your non-bottle-holding hand while (2) simultaneously pushing upward with your index/fulcrum finger and ensuring it's wedged under the cap. This will keep the fulcrum steady as downward force is applied to the lighter by

your other hand. You don't want to push upward TOO hard, but if you don't do anything, none of this is going to work, and Dave is just going to want his lighter back before you break it.

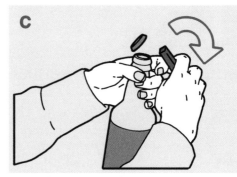

Pop and welcome applause.

STEP 4: Play around with the pressure on both hands a bit, but when you get it right, the bottle cap should pop right off. Bottle caps can tend to be disagreeable, however, so sometimes you'll only be able to wedge up a little bit of the cap. If that happens, don't consider yourself a failure just yet, and rotate the bottle a quarter of an inch or so, then repeat. You shouldn't have to do this more than two or three times before your beer has been freed from the clutches of cap-dom. Of course, if you get it off in one flourish-filled, pop-accompanied shot, people will have considerably more respect for you.

STEP 5: Drink your beer. It's crucial to not forget this part amid all the excitement.

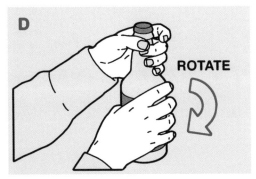

If you keep turning slightly and nudging the cap up, you'll be good eventually.

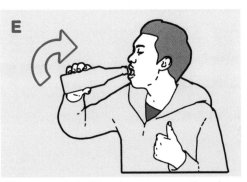

All beers taste better when you open them in an impressive fashion.

METHOD 3:

17 WEDDING RING TO THE RESCUE

The best way to squeeze some ancillary value out of your jewelry

The best part about being married, of course, is the eternal bliss that comes from waking up next to your best friend, confidant, and true counterpart, every single morning (Hi, Rebecca!!). The second-best part, also of course, is getting to look really cool while opening beer bottles with your wedding ring. Of course you can also use your class ring, Super Bowl ring, One Ring to Rule Them All, etc.

WHAT YOU'LL NEED: One bottle of beer, one wedding ring (on finger)

Make that jewelry earn its keep.

STEP 1: Presuming you wear your wedding ring on your left hand, grab the bottle with your right hand, and place your left palm on the bottle's neck.

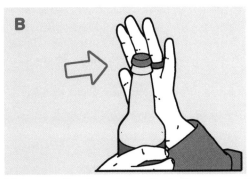

Make sure the ring catches the bottom edge of the cap.

STEP 2: Curl your ring finger over the top of the bottle cap, ensuring you lodge the top of the piece of jewelry that represents your eternal devotion underneath one or two of the bottom ridges of the cap.

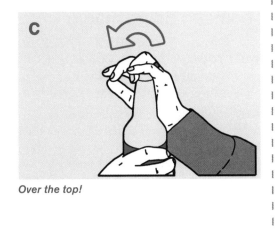

Over the top!

STEP 3: Roll your entire left hand over the top in as straight a motion as possible while keeping pressure against the cap, and it should pop right off.

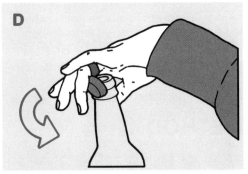

Like everything else in life, it's all about the follow-through.

STEP 4: Drink your beer, and silently thank the plumber who managed to find your ring after rooting around in the drain for 25 minutes that one time.

Another satisfied Beer Hacks customer

IMPORTANT DETAIL STUFF: This theoretically could work for any ring, excluding ones made of plastic and delicious hard candy. HOWEVER, you do need to know that the cap's aluminum is harder than traditionally favored wedding band materials such as silver and gold, which means there exists the possibility of denting and scratching. Materials like platinum and certainly titanium should see no ill effects, and if you somehow have a wedding band made of tungsten, oh MAN, can you feel good and safe about things.

METHOD 4:

18 USING A PIECE OF PAPER (SERIOUSLY)

Perhaps as close as you'll ever come to doing magic

This one would double as a fantastic bar bet to score yourself a free round from unsuspecting rubes, if only bars would stop being so damn hospitable and opening your beers for you. Shame. It can still function as a fun, surprising showstopper, though, and here's how you do it.

WHAT YOU'LL NEED: One bottle of beer, one piece of paper (try to ensure it's the standard 8.5" × 11" notebook size, at least)

STEP 1: When somebody finds themselves without a means to open their bottle of beer, look around the room as if you're searching for a bottle opener, then, after failing to find one, look like a light bulb went off and say, "Actually, does anyone have a piece of paper?"

Don't skimp on the theatrics.

STEP 2: Field a chorus of doubtful questioning and people calling you crazy, because their minds are weak.

Get down to folding.

STEP 3: Piece of paper in hand, use it to make some slashing gestures with the bottle cap/neck as the target. Look frustrated when that doesn't work, and while doing so, fold the piece of paper in half, and then in half again, and then again, until the paper's stacked thickness will allow it to fold no more. You may remember from a more grade-school-ish challenge that you theoretically can only fold a piece of paper seven times. No need to attempt to break world records; six or seven folds should do the trick here.

And then fold some more.

STEP 4: Paper folded, say, "Oh wait—let me try this," then proceed to use the exact same principles laid out in the Lighter Move method, with the folded paper subbing in for the lighter. The folding should have rendered the paper stiff enough to be usable as a lever. The trick itself should have made your audience believe that you are capable of literally anything.

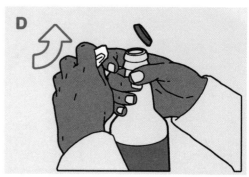

Magic is real.

METHOD 5:

19 THE *DOOR JAMB* MOVE

Doors: finally good for something

It's worth saying right up front that if all other options have failed, this is absolutely a viable one, but you're getting into territory in which your beer is going to spill or spray a little bit. But sometimes you just need one, dammit.

WHAT YOU'LL NEED: One bottle of beer, one door jamb with a traditional strike plate—that's the metal thing that the latch clicks into (bet you didn't know it was called that)

STEP 1: Take your bottle and hold it sideways so the top of the bottle is creating slightly less than a right angle to the door jamb.

Some door jambs will allow you to NOT go sideways, but this works, too.

STEP 2: Wedge the ridges of the cap into the strike plate, fiddling with the placement until they click right in.

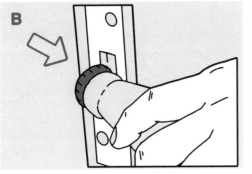

Just be aware you may lose some beer.

STEP 3: While constantly applying pressure toward the strike plate, simultaneously push down on the bottle, and the cap should begin to bend upward and open the beer.

But hey . . .

STEP 4: Ensure that you do all this very quickly, so you don't casually pour a bottle of beer on the floor, unless, for some reason, that's why you wanted it open in the first place.

METHOD 6:

20 *OPEN A BEER* WITH *ANOTHER BEER*

And pray the universe doesn't collapse in on itself

While this is both the most desperate and most showy of all these methods, it's also rooted in the principles behind the Lighter Move method. Just get the ridge of one cap (which will be your lever) under the other, create that fulcrum, and make it happen.

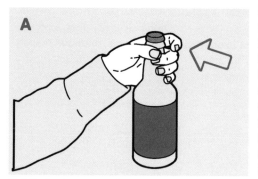

A

Get that grip prepared.

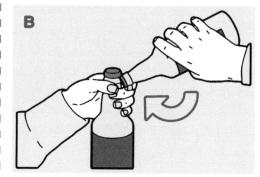

B

Wedge and apply upward pressure.

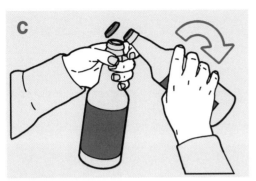

C

Pop, POP!!

D

Celebrate with a drink.

METHOD 7:

21 YOUR *TEETH*

WHAT YOU'LL NEED: One bottle of beer, one mouth full of teeth, one very skilled and available periodontist

STEP 1: For real? You really want to do this? Just figure out how to do the lighter one, please.

You really need to value your bicuspids.

METHOD 8:

22 JUST *TWIST IT* OFF

WHAT YOU'LL NEED: One beer . . . with a twist-off cap

STEP 1: Absolutely never do this, because all the other methods we just ran through are way, way more fun.

STEP 2: So, use one of them instead.

Pictured: the most dangerously unimaginative person in the world.

How to
Store Your Beer, Smartly

Some beers (stouts, barleywines, and other high-ABV types) can keep their flavor for years or even improve with age. Others (hazy IPAs, especially) can lose their burst of flavor within a handful of weeks. But no matter how long you're planning on keeping your beers around before enjoying the hell out of them, they need to be stored—correctly.

23 *BEER CANS AND BOTTLES* SHOULD ALWAYS BE STORED UPRIGHT

This simple hack will keep your beers delicious for as long as possible.

Think about it. "It" being a beer bottle standing up. How much beer is touching the air-filled non-beer area? Only as much as the neck is wide, so not very much at all. Then think about a beer bottle lying on its side. Well, now there's all sorts of contact with that air—the affected section runs down the length of the entire bottle.

Turns out there's oxygen in air! But unlike you (hopefully), beer despises oxygen, and any prolonged exposure to said evil O_2 causes the alcohol and flavor compounds within your beer to react badly, creating a stale taste that will only get worse and worse as that exposure continues. So, limiting the amount of beer surface area contacting oxygen is crucial

to keeping things good and fresh and wonderful. Even if you consider yourself to be composed of one hundred percent beer, I'll still make a strong recommendation that you continue to breathe, at least a few times daily.

Join the Upright Bottle Brigade.

24 USE A *BINDER CLIP TO STACK YOUR* BEERS, PYRAMID-STYLE, IN THE FRIDGE

Although this structure probably won't last as long as the Egyptians'

At some point, we've all done it: Jacked some office supplies from work just because they were there, and they were free, and dammit, you're gonna get that place to compensate you like you deserve, even if it's in Wite-Out.

Luckily for you, those giant binder

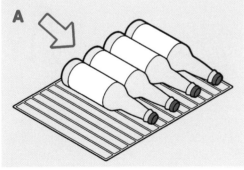

These will roll around all mischievously.

These will not.

clips you pocketed can have far more of a purpose than just being something to play with until you snap your finger in them. This one's really easy. Just (1) figure out how many beers will form the base of your pyramid (three to five, most likely), and lay them down on the fridge rack, then (2) open up the alligator mouth of that binder clip and have it eat a couple of rails on the rack, so its open end is facing up. If you have lined it all up correctly, the clip will act as a brake to keep the bottom beers from rolling away when you stack more on top of them, and more on top of THOSE, and so on.

"But the last hack," you may say, "just told me to store all my beers upright, and this isn't that." First off, thanks for reading linearly. Second, you are correct! But sometimes, reasons arise to just jam

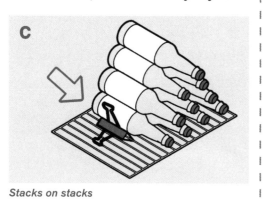

Stacks on stacks

your fridge as full as you possibly can, in whatever direction the cans and bottles must go to maximize that jamming, safe in the knowledge that the beers will go quickly. Like, say, if a bunch of thirsty friends are coming over for a cookout (in which case, see hacks 37 and 38 for two essential beer-based grilling recipes). Or you invented a new game called Beer Tetris.

A couple of important caveats: Not all refrigerators have the kind of grated shelving that will support this kind of move. And, as the next couple hacks will tell you, this approach to beer storage should sometimes be discarded in favor of letting all your bottles stand up tall like good, proud bottles with excellent posture, BECAUSE . . .

25 YOU REALLY DON'T NEED TO *BLOW MONEY ON AN EXPENSIVE BEER FRIDGE*

Spend the savings on beer!

While some companies want you to overspend on a higher-end, beer-specific fridge, most of the pricier models are for wine, the alcoholic beverage that's just too classy to be hacked. And of course they have the cool glass door so you can clearly see that it is NOT, in fact, a dedicated POLLY-O string cheese fridge (a common misperception).

A NO NO

Don't succumb.

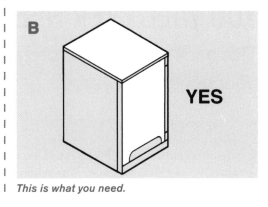

B YES

This is what you need.

You do not need one of these fancy refrigerators. Neither do the wine drinkers, really, but let them overspend on appliances and ribbed turtlenecks; it's all part of their "thing." What you DO need depends on how much beer space you require and how that measures up against the beer-space-time continuum.

If you've generally got not-massive overall amounts of beer and that stock turns over fairly frequently, good work! Beer is for drinking, and you're doing that. You could invest in one of those college-boy mini-fridges and be juuuuust fine. Good ones can be had for under $200, which is much more efficient and probably also cheaper than having to replace the ice in your garbage can every six hours or so.

26 HOW TO *CREATE THE CHEAPEST, BIGGEST BEER FRIDGE* YOU WILL EVER NEED

This hack's definitely a project, but you'll be reaping the beer benefits for years.

If you've become more of a collector/ hoarder (either is fine) and need more space, an entirely new fridge can feel a little out of reach, cost wise. Plus, when jammed full of shoulder-to-shoulder beers, a fridge might not even be strong enough to keep everything as cold as you need to still have respect for yourself.

Luckily for you, there's a hack answer to both problems:

STEP 1: Go on Craigslist and search for a freezer. Not a chest freezer, but a stand-up jobber with a door that basically looks like a fridge. Look every day! Eventually, some poor soul who just had to close their mac-and-cheese-only restaurant named It IS Easy Being Cheesy (which clearly turned out to not be true) will put one up there for basically free. Then it's just on you to figure out how to pick the thing up (I recommend not with your hands—they're heavy!) and get it back home.

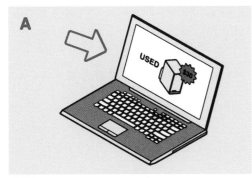

The internet was built for this.

STEP 2: Once you've got your freezer in your living room, any reasonable person with whom you live will tell you to put it in the garage or basement. Do that.

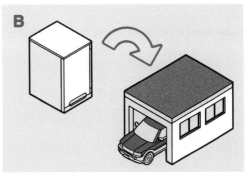

Not to scale (unless you found an impressively large freezer)

STEP 3: Purchase a "Digital Temperature Controller Outlet Thermostat" (one costs $30 or so), which is a device that plugs into any outlet and will, via magic, regulate the temperature of your new freezer-that-will-actually-be-a-fridge to ensure that nothing gets *toooo* cold. As a bonus, freezers have better insulation, which means you can turn your electricity savings into even more beer. Set it to around 45 degrees, and guess what? You just got yourself a giant beer fridge that will be able to cool any size stash, and you are now addicted to the used appliance section of Craigslist.

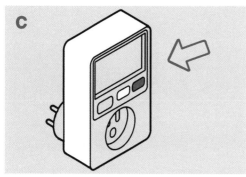

Technology is your friend.

Set it and forget it! Except don't forget the beer.

Cleaning Things
with Beer

For most people, beer is something that gets everything dirty—it spills on your shirt, the floor, or your gigantic novelty beanbag chair that looks like a cheeseburger. But the true beer lover knows that for every single item that beer temporarily ruined, there's something else that's just sitting there, begging for beer to fix it. For instance, you can . . .

27 CLEAN YOUR GOLD JEWELRY WITH BEER AND A SOFT CLOTH

The best deserves the best, right?

So long as your eternal partner was kind enough to slip a solid gold or gold-plated ring onto your finger before you headed off to the reception to drink a ton of beer, you can return it (and, surely, your marriage!) to its initial shine with a little bit of light beer and a soft cloth. Just get the cloth slightly wet with the brew, then buff, buff, buff, before wiping things down with a different, beer-free cloth.

An alternate move is to drop it into a glass of beer and let it soak for a bit before polishing, although hospital records from the gastrointestinal unit indicate that literally every single person who has tried this has completely forgotten about it and simply finished their beer.

The nice thing about this and other beer-based cleaning deployments is that "good" beer actually cleans things up WORSE—you want to use something very straightforward and very cheap.

Just pop it in there, then polish it up.

28 SHINE UP YOUR POTS

Very helpful when your dishwasher has been sandbagging it

The reason the gold jewelry maneuver (hack 27) works is because of beer's light acidity—impactful enough to get some work done but not so strong that an evil mastermind will want to come over and slowly lower you into a vat of it. Although, if he did, since it IS beer, maybe he wouldn't be so evil after all. Just . . . misunderstood.

That same acidity can claw some of the piled-up grime and grease off that pot that you left sitting in the sink for weeks, in the hopes that a compulsively clean burglar would break into your house. But he never seems to, does he? For this one, you just get a rag good and soaked, and polish away. If you want to drop some beer in first and let it soak for a minute, or even better, employ the "some for the pot, some for me" move, nobody will yell at you (probably). Just be sure to rinse everything out with regular old water at the end. The trick works on copper pots especially well, but it can be used on everything other than cast iron—which will want to soak up beer like it does everything else—or anything with a nonstick surface.

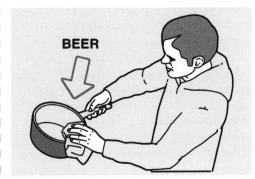

Dirty finally met its match.

29 GIVE YOUR TABLE A LUSTER *THAT WOULD MAKE MR. CLEAN LOOK LIKE PIG-PEN*

(Not in terms of musculature, just hygiene)

Have you ever spilled beer on your table at a party, then considered getting a cleaning product for exactly zero seconds, calmly wiped it off with a paper towel, and proclaimed it "better than new"? Of course you have. The great part is that you weren't even lying to yourself. The brew works to give the wood a burst of shine and might even restore some of the faded color, if you're lucky. Flat beer is best here, and again, the cheaper and simpler, the better. If instead of having a nice coat of something or other on it your table is raw and unfinished, this isn't recommended, although it does sound like you have a very cool table.

Will your table smell a little like old ale for the next couple days? Yes, of course—you just rubbed beer all over it. But you bought yourself some time to go buy that furniture polish spray.

BEER

Don't forget to save some for yourself.

30 *CLEAN COFFEE STAINS* OUT OF YOUR CARPET

Because you'll never stop spilling that coffee, will you?

Coffee, basically the contrapositive of beer but every bit as important, tends to spill itself in the worst places. Carpets are high on that list, and while the traditional Keep Dabbing Sparkling Water Basically Forever trick can certainly work in the right circumstances (most notably when you get to it fast enough), so can beer.

Unlike some of the other cleaning tricks that require you to walk around frat houses the morning after a party to find a flat one, this time around you're gonna want a fresher beer with the carbonation still rocking. And PLEASE, nothing dark—if you do that, you'll only need a lighter beer to clean out the imperial stout you just sacrificed. Then, instead of dabbing, get in there and rub like you've never rubbed before (except that one time at Head Rub Fest '06, but hey, situationally, you had to), and repeat until it's all good and gone.

Rub it good.

31 THE ONE YOU WON'T BELIEVE: *RINSE YOUR HAIR WITH THE STUFF*

Introducing: the beer-hair day

Let's get this right out front: You do not want to WASH your hair with beer. That's still the job of shampoo. Maybe even Pert Plus, if you're strapped for time but still want to condition. But once you've washed, pouring a glass or so of flat beer into your mane and working it around can do all sorts of stuff. While everyone's hair is different (Think about it: Does YOUR hair look like Zac Efron's? If you answered yes, thank you for buying this book, Zac Efron.), reduced greasiness, added luster, and general controllability are some of the benefits of beer-hair.

This sounds crazy, of course. It's like someone endured a hazing ritual, then showed up at school the next day, and everyone immediately wanted to date them and pet their hair. But guess what?

Catherine Zeta-Jones does it (although she also works in some honey, because she's fancier than this book can possibly hope to recommend). And her hair is legit enough to star in movies opposite Corbin Bernsen, so you know it works.

Cannot stress it enough: Catherine Zeta-Jones does this.

Other Ways
Your Beer Can Help You Around the House

As already evidenced, beer's versatility is one of the driving forces behind *Beer Hacks*, and it extends well beyond making things magically clean. Whenever you're looking to justify the purchase of more beer than you initially intended, just refer to this section, and bathe in complete and utter validation.

32 HELP YOUR GARDEN THRIVE BY *SETTING BEER-BASED TRAPS FOR SLUGS*

Get this one down, and you'll be a subsistence farmer in no time.

Slugs are shameless, hungry, and willing to go after just about anything you've got in about any size garden, including leaves, seedlings, fruits, vegetables, and slime-despising bare human feet.

Enter beer. Slugs love beer even more than they love carving holes through your rutabaga. And if you rig a beer-based trap correctly, the slugs will fall in and be unable to slink their way out.

STEP 1: Grab a sturdy plastic cup and dig a hole in your garden that can accommodate its circumference.

A

It's good to get your hands a little dirty.

STEP 2: Place the cup into the hole but NOT all the way down—you want the rim of the cup to be an inch or so above the soil.

STEP 3: Fill it three-quarters of the way up with light beer.

Fill it up, but not TOO high.

STEP 4: Watch slugs get interested in the beer, slime their way up the side of the cup, have a few sips of the beer, and then fall in, never to slug around again. Will this get every single slug in the world? Of course not; even slugs are teetotalers sometimes, plus they need to get fairly close to the trap to realize there's delicious beer in it. So you'll need find your own personal balance between fewer slugs and a yard full of nearly buried Solo cups.

Suckers!

33 AND IT'LL *STOP FRUIT FLIES, TOO*

Because even flies know beer is more desirable than fruit.

Obviously, any creature that consumes any amount of beer will immediately fall in love with it. Which puts you in a fantastic position to lure those pesky fruit flies into a beer oasis they'll never want to leave.

STEP 1: Start with a mason jar. If you have to empty out that tricolor sand-scape you made in third grade, that's totally okay.

STEP 2: Grab a hammer, a decent-size nail, and the metal lid to the mason jar. Then ram the nail through the lid to make four or five holes, and screw it back on. A drill can work here, too.

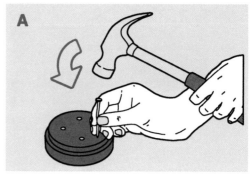

A

Nailed it.

STEP 3: Fill up the jar about halfway with any beer—the cheaper the better, as it turns out that fruit flies actually aren't true beer connoisseurs and will dig pretty much anything.

STEP 4: Check out those flies zipping right through those holes, then never coming out. It's basically like if you put Barney from *The Simpsons* into a lager-filled aquarium; he wouldn't be in a hurry to go much of anywhere.

Fill halfway or so.

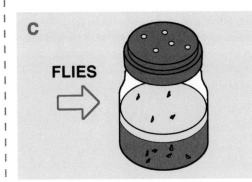

FLIES

Beer: Always more appealing than fruit.

34 AND IT WILL AT LEAST *DISTRACT BEES*

An easy trick for reducing bee-based panic at your cookouts

While it may not lure them to their ultimate demise, bees definitely get interested in the sugars in beer and decide to devote a little time to checking it out. The simple move here is to position a bunch of small cups of beer as a perimeter around where you're hanging outside, which will at least give you a fighting chance against the ever-building swarm.

We may never win the war against bees, but taking a battle ain't bad.

35 BUT UNFORTUNATELY *MOSQUITOS LOVE PEOPLE* WHO DRINK BEER, SO . . .

You have to take the good (beer) with the bad (mosquitos craving your blood).

The short story here is, researchers have found that even one beer will make its consumer more attractive to mosquitoes. Which basically confirms that mosquitos are more similar to people in the bar at last call than anyone previously realized.

Nobody has really pinned down the

It's worth it.

reason why, but the main thing is: They're coming for you, so wear sleeves and long pants whenever possible, and throw on some deep-woods bug spray. And then *juuuuuuuuuuusssssst* keep drinking your beer.

36 WANT BETTER SLEEP? *HOPS WILL HELP.*

No, not the ones inside your beer.

You may not have needed a doctor to tell you that beer makes you sleepy, but plenty of them will. And they'll also tell you that it's the properties of the hops that aid in getting you all good and rested, by affecting your melatonin receptors—which was first noticed when the fieldworkers who harvested hop plants would be far more drowsy than people harvesting other crops and sometimes would even fall asleep on the job. There are a couple of ways to aid your sleep cycles with everyone's favorite little cone-shaped flowers.

PICK UP A nice big bag at a local brewing supply shop, or order some from any number of sites online. Then rub your

DRIED HOPS

You'll need "leaf" hops—not pellets.

Just a drop or two will do.

pillowcases with hops, and their aromatics will find their way to your nostrils, and then your brain, and then you will sleep like a baby, which also had its pillowcase rubbed down with hops.

DOSE YOURSELF WITH a little hops extract, which you can find at health food stores, or, you know, on the internet. Also, a lot of people who spend their waking hours thinking about how other people sleep recommend mixing that with root extract (300 milligrams to 600 millgrams, max) for maximum effectiveness. The Germans love it! Really, they do.

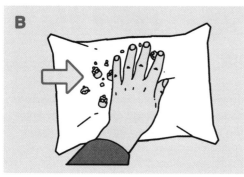

Rub-a-dub-hop . . .

The Only Two
Beer-Based
Food Recipes
You Really Need

Beer-battered fish. Beef and stout stew. Beer cheese. Beer bread. IPA toast. All of these are wonderful and worthy recipes, even the one I just made up. But in the end, there are truly only two dishes based in beer with which you need to arm yourself. They're simple, they're outstanding, they can feed a small group, and most important, they refuse to go light on the beer.

37 MAKE *A VERY DELICIOUS BEER CAN CHICKEN*

This is a classic recipe for a reason: It works.

Shoving a can of beer up a chicken's butt imbues it with some beery flavor, ensures the bird comes out good and moist, and also acts as a stand to keep everything in the right place on the grill.

WHAT YOU'LL NEED: One whole chicken (preferably 4 to 5 pounds), one 12-ounce can of domestic pilsner or light beer, salt, pepper, a charcoal or gas grill

STEP 1: Get your grill going. The huge thing to remember here—this chicken MUST cook via indirect heat. Which means that if you've got charcoal, you're gonna wanna get it fired up and hot like you normally would, but once it's ready, move it to one side of the grill, because the chicken's going on the other. With gas, you'll just ensure the burners directly under the chicken aren't on (and ensure the other burners are) and try to dial it in to right around 300°F.

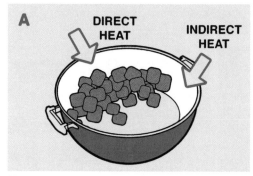

Keep the coals consolidated for that indirect heat.

STEP 2: Rub down both the inside and outside of your chicken with the salt and pepper. You can also buy or create a spice rub, but honestly, salt and pepper are all most of the expertly grilled meats REALLY need.

Don't be shy.

STEP 3: Time to put the beer in the chicken. As mentioned above, you want a light beer or domestic pilsner, and not anything one bit fancier: PBR or Bud Heavy work great. And you don't want your beer can to be totally full when it goes into the bird, so pour out half of it. WAIT, WAIT, WAIT!! You didn't really do that, did you? You're the owner of a book called *Beer Hacks*—drink half of that thing, dammit. Then shove the half-full (optimism!) can into the cavity.

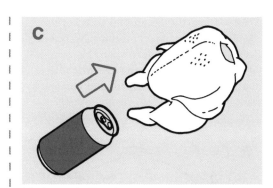

It's honestly like they were designed to fit beer cans.

STEP 4: As mentioned before, the beer can is as much for stability as it is for flavor. Ensure the can is at the exact right height to allow the two legs of the chicken to also touch the grill grates, effectively forming a tripod that will anchor the whole thing in place as it cooks.

Keeping it upright is the whole key.

STEP 5: Close the lid and let that sucker cook for an hour and 15 minutes. No peeking!! Seriously, don't you dare open that lid—it'll let all sorts of heat escape and might also disrupt your chicken tripod, and you don't want either of those things to happen.

Close that top.

STEP 6: When your timer goes off, use a meat thermometer to ensure the chicken breast is at least 165°F, then take it off the grill, pop that can out, carve (or just rip apart with your hungry, hungry hands), and enjoy.

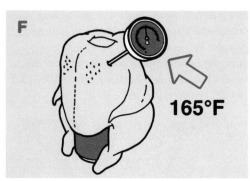

165°F

You can go higher, but you definitely shouldn't go lower.

BONUS BACON STEP: After you season your bird, wrap three to four pieces of raw bacon around the chicken to cover the bulk of its body, fasten the strips with some toothpicks, and then shove that can in. Bacon never hurt anything, and it certainly isn't about to start now.

38 BEER + BRATWURST =
A TASTE OF WISCONSIN SUMMER

The official food of one of the United States' beeriest states

I went to college in Wisconsin. People always associate the state with cheese—whenever I saw a friend or corny uncle during the years I was in school, "How much cheese are you eating?" was the not terribly original question/joke. And yes, cheese was consumed, quite often.

But beer brats are the food that I find most defines the state, its people, and their famous appetites. I'm pretty sure I never encountered a single time when meat was grilled that brats weren't over the flames, too. And most of those times, they weren't just torn out of the package and hurled on the grill—any good Wisconsinite knows that if you don't boil the brats in beer first, you're barely even eating brats. It's like, in Wisconsin, even a sausage deserves one last big beer-filled afternoon of fun before it goes out. Plus, they end up tasting way better. Now, of course, you can do this with hot dogs as well, but hey—this is an ode to the great beer-loving state of Wisconsin, where brats rule the cookout.

WHAT YOU'LL NEED: A deep pot or dutch oven, a grill, five beers, an onion, some truly hearty long buns, and a package of bratwurst. Your best shot outside of Wisconsin is finding some Johnsonvilles, and honestly, you shouldn't dare look for anything even a touch fancier.

STEP 1: Get the grill going, then slice that onion and throw it in the pot on your stove, along with four beers. The fifth one is for you.

STEP 2: Take that to a boil, then toss in the brats, and reduce the heat to medium. Keep it there for about 10 minutes, maybe 12, then pull out the brats, but keep the onions going on slightly lower heat.

Boiling beer is oddly satisfying.

STEP 3: Your brats should be cooked, but they aren't finished, no sir, they are not. Put them on the grill for a minute or two and then turn them and let 'em sit for the same time. The goal here is to get some nice char on the brats and to get that casing ready to make a big ol' snap when you bite into it.

The bratwurst in its natural environment

STEP 4: Get your brat into a bun, fish some onions out of the beer stock and throw them on top, then add mustard and enjoy. NEVER ADD KETCHUP. Never. Just don't do it. My god, Wisconsinites can get pretty serious about that part.

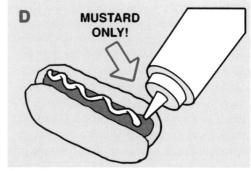

Cook until there's at least a bit of char, or plenty of it, if you like that.

MUSTARD ONLY!

Crucial

Four

Beautiful, Easy Beer Cocktails

Nick Bennett

Certain occasions just call for a cocktail. Luckily, those cocktails can themselves call for a beer as a key ingredient. I asked my good buddy Nick Bennett to work up four that can get you through multiple occasions. Nick is head bartender at Porchlight in New York City and has a beautiful mustache. Unless, of course, it's one of those days he has a beautiful beard or beautiful muttonchops. Take it away, Nick . . .

39 *AMARO* AND *BEER* COCKTAIL

Two simple ingredients make for a remarkable taste transformation.

This is probably the easiest application to upgrade your beer game at home by adding some unique bitterness and sweetness, and it can be adjusted to your preferred taste any way that you want. The only thing that you really need to know is the most basic of bartending skills: pouring things into other things.

YOU WILL NEED:

12-ounce bottle or can of your preferred pilsner or lager

1 ounce Italian Amaro (I would recommend one with a little citrus to it, like Montenegro or Averna, though a little pine and smoke from Braulio would be nice on a cold day.)

A pint glass or Collins glass

PILSNER (OR LAGER)

1 OUNCE AMARO

Simple, delicious, effective

HOW YOU MAKE IT:

1. Pour the Amaro into the glass, then fill the rest with the beer.

2. Or: Take a healthy sip from the can or bottle, then simply pour the Amaro directly into the vessel.

40 BLACK VELVET

Sometimes a perfect pint can be made even better.

Put the black and tan to shame. This beauty first appeared in London in the 1860s and will help you extend the life of any bottle of Champagne—especially helpful if you're hosting friends/freeloaders.

YOU WILL NEED:

One 12-ounce can or bottle of Guinness

One bottle of Champagne (or a sparkling wine if you don't feel like splurging)

A Champagne flute

A spoon

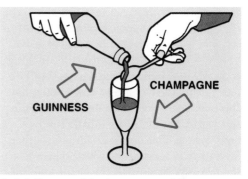

Polish those upside-down-spoon skills.

HOW YOU MAKE IT:

1. Fill your glass halfway with Champagne.

2. Slowly pour the Guinness over the back of a spoon on top of the Champagne (adding the Guinness last will create a very visually cool layering effect). That's literally it.

41 *CITRON SHANDY*

How to make summer even more refreshing

While you may love them, the hoppiness of American IPAs tends to be too aggressive for me. But I enjoy making cocktails that build on the flavors that I *do* like, mostly the citrus and piney notes, like this one. There are all kinds of shandies in this world, but many are a little too "one note" for me. This version adds a few other layers to the cocktail—the bitterness of the IPA is backed up by the citrus and the juniper of the two spirits. It also packs a little more of a punch.

YOU WILL NEED:

1 ounce Bittermens Citron Sauvage

1 ounce London dry gin
(like Tanqueray or Beefeater)

One 12-ounce American IPA

A Collins glass

Ice

Cool ice cubes are recommended.

HOW YOU MAKE IT:

1. Fill your Collins glass with ice.

2. Add the Citron Sauvage and gin, and give them a quick stir to mix.

3. Top with the IPA and give it another stir to incorporate the flavors.

42 HIGHLIFE GIMLET

This one's a little more complicated, but oh, so worth it.

There is no law stating that every beer cocktail has to be simply "topped with beer." I asked attorneys. There are plenty of other ways to incorporate beer into a cocktail; one is turning it into a syrup. Scared? Just remember that the simple syrup is only sugar and water, so why not try replacing the water with beer? Of course, I'm going to make it less simple. But it'll be worth it.

YOU WILL NEED:

2 ounces gin

¾ ounce fresh lime juice

¾ ounce Simple Beer Syrup
(read on for recipe)

A coupe glass (No, not a drinking vessel made from a two-door Honda Civic. It's the saucer-like, instead of flute-style, type of Champagne glass.)

One cocktail shaker

A measuring jigger

Ice

But first, let's make the Simple Beer Syrup.

THIS REQUIRES:

8 ounces of lager or pilsner

½ cup raw sugar

2 whole cardamom pods

1 whole cinnamon stick

Pinch of salt

Throw all of the ingredients in a small saucepan and bring to a boil, being careful not to let it foam over. Turn the heat down to low and simmer until the liquid has started to reduce (become far thicker and less beery), then remove from the heat and strain out the spices. Allow it to cool, and you'll have approximately one cup.

And now, how you make the cocktail:

1. Using your jigger, measure out the gin, lime juice, and Simple Beer Syrup into a cocktail shaker over ice.

2. Shake vigorously for 20 to 30 seconds.

3. Strain into a coupe glass and blow your damn mind.

Enjoy the spoils.

Crucial

Beer Life Hacks

For many an enlightened individual, beer is life. So it stands to reason that a book like this one must outline a handful of beer life hacks: little bits of advice to help guide you through a range of various beer-involving situations. What do you need to know to enjoy Oktoberfest most completely? How, pray tell, should you be drinking them in the shower? And once you get good at that, where can you go to actually bathe in beer? Bone up on these, and get prepared to do beer better.

43 *HOW TO ORDER BEER* AT A PROFESSIONAL SPORTING EVENT

How to save time, money, and your relationship with your seatmates

Drinking beer at sporting events is not only an American tradition, in some cases it's basically required—the two most notable being (1) if your team is terrible; and (2) all baseball games in general.

But there is only one right way to order those beers, summed up by two simple rules.

RULE 1: ALWAYS, ALWAYS, ALWAYS GET THE BIGGEST BEER THEY SELL.

Beer at any pro game is going to be overpriced; they have succeeded in capturing you, and therefore, can charge essentially whatever they want. But in almost all cases, your cost per ounce will decline as the size of the cup goes up. Get the big one, so you can feel better about yourself. Do not under any circumstances worry about how you'll feel about yourself tomorrow. That would just play into their hands.

Go big or go . . . back to the bar, far too often.

RULE 2: ORDER TWO BEERS INSTEAD OF ONE.

There's nothing worse than getting out of your seat at a game. You have to awkwardly ask everyone else in your row to get up to let you by, you temporarily block dozens of people's view of their heroes, and your shoe soles will attract many, many peanut shells that will inevitably later end up, somehow, in your hair. How to mitigate all this? Get two beers, and therefore, get up less.

This is especially important as it gets closer to last call.

BONUS TIP: Ask for lids so that you don't splash three dollars and seventy-five cents' worth of suds all over your row mates, who already like you less than they do the opposing team.

44 THREE CRUCIAL RULES FOR *BACHELOR PARTY BEER CONSUMPTION*

The best bachelor parties are as much hard work as they are fun, but follow these simple frameworks and you'll be in great shape.

RULE 1: For every beer you drink, also drink a glass of water. Now, this takes a SIGNIFICANT amount more concentration and focus and commitment than you could possibly imagine. But say you're going to do it, and then just do it. Tell yourself the reason is so you can more readily drink additional beer tomorrow (and water, of course). Will you have to head to the bathroom more? Yes! But sometimes they have funny things written on the wall, or a cool, jet-powered hand-dryer, so it's worth it.

A very necessary pair

RULE 2: Before dinner, only drink light-ish beer. Let's say under 6% ABV. There's a reason they call it "session beer"—when you're in the midst of a very long one, it won't cause said session to prematurely end. But at dinner and after, whatever goes.

Be judicious, and the rewards will be great indeed.

RULE 3: Do not attempt to thwart Rule 2 by eating dinner at 1:45 p.m.

45 SOME REALLY IMPORTANT *BEER PONG STUFF*

Tips for keeping yourself healthy, honorable, and awake while playing the ultimate beer sport

Always, always, always use a water cup to rinse the Ping-Pong balls you're playing with before you throw. The beer in those triangularly arranged cups in front of you? You're going to drink it. The floor you're stepping on with your shoes that have also, at some point, whether you want to admit it or not, stepped in at least trace amounts of old dog poop? The balls will roll around on it. Use the water so you can feel okay about drinking the beer/don't contract giardia.

SOME PEOPLE PLAY with rules stating that if your team wins, your vanquished opponents have to stand in front of you and drink the still-full cups of beer that they didn't hit. This is ridiculous. Getting

LOSER   WINNER

Always wash your balls.

Drinking = winning

to drink beer is a privilege, and you should take every possible advantage of that privilege. Plus, drinking it makes you a benevolent conqueror. Everyone loves those.

LIGHT, LOW-ABV, SESSION-ABLE beer is your only option. Filling those Solo cups with an imperial porter may sound like a total badass move, but the whole idea is to win, and then play again, and win, and then play again, and . . . just use the light stuff.

There will be plenty of other opportunities to be a hero.

46 HOW TO *MASTER THE SHOWER BEER*

Get prepared to spend a lot more time in there.

Ever since the visionary Mr. Harry American Standard invented the showerhead, inspired people have been drinking beers while simultaneously covering themselves in other kinds of suds. And while this author would never advocate for something like building the practice into your normal pre-work routine, there are occasions when a shower beer is the only sensible route to go: say, while running late getting ready to go out on a Saturday night, or while running perfectly on time getting ready to go out on a Saturday night and just wanting a damn beer.

The guidelines of shower beer drinking are detailed below:

AS FOR WHERE to secure your beer, you need to think about a combination of height (to avoid water splashing in) and distance from the showerhead (for the same reason). So, while they're temptingly excellent at holding cylindrical objects, those shampoo caddies that attach to the showerhead neck are, sadly, out.

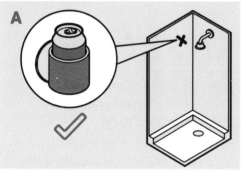

This is why they have walls in showers.

I UNFORTUNATELY CAN'T tell you exactly where to place your beer—every shower is different, and I haven't been into your house to see yours, because that would be weird (although potentially very helpful in this instance). So eye it up and look for a ledge, or railing, or something that's supposed to hold something else but would also accommodate a beer can very nicely. The floor is always a very bad idea. Thoughtful companies have also created suction-cup shower beer holders or sleeves that you can invest in, once you realize this is the lifestyle for you. Just Google away.

ALWAYS CANS, NEVER bottles. It doesn't take a ton of imagination to picture the vastly differing worst-case scenarios for either if you drop your beer or it slips, which it almost definitely will at some point in your shower beer career—I mean, things are wet and soapy, and you're such a shower beer novice that you're researching how to drink one in a book.

No glass!

STAY IN THERE up to three times as long as normal, for maximum enjoyment of both the shower and the beer.

ONLY ONE BEER allowed per shower. I mean, we still live in a society here.

Remain sane. One beer per shower.

47 HOW TO *SURVIVE A BEER FESTIVAL*

Yes, they're a helluva time, but things can get away from you quick if you're not careful.

These days you can find beer festivals filling up weekend leisure time just about anywhere, and they are wonderful: Dozens or sometimes even hundreds of breweries set up stands everywhere from open fields to Grand Central Terminal, and as you walk around to each for hours on end, they just give you tiny little cups of beer, over and over and over! Beer festivals are also dangerous: Dozens or sometimes even hundreds of breweries just give you tiny little cups of beer, over and over and over. But approached properly, they will deliver everything you wanted, and you can leave as a reasonably functional human. Just follow the tips on the next pages:

REMEMBER THAT THOSE TINY CUPS ADD UP:
At a beer festival you are generally
supposed to get a 2- to 4-ounce pour. The
glasses, though, are much bigger than
that, and you'll often get poured extra,
sometimes more than half a can's worth.
Because of the situation—More beer
everywhere!! Somewhat limited time!—you
may feel compelled to down it and motor
over to the next tap. That's fine, sometimes.
But at least periodically, remember to
take your time. Wander around to scout
things before drinking, get a free pair of
sunglasses just for signing yourself up for
wind-powered energy, maybe swing by the
live band that's honestly not very good
but is still a live band. Breathe. You won't
regret it. At these things, there is quite
literally always more beer.

Great beer is worth a search.

EMBRACE THE LINE. Lines and humans are
natural enemies. At a beer festival, you will
see a line and do everything to avoid it so
you can get more beer more quickly. Rage
against this urge. Long lines (1) almost
always have better beer at the end of them
(that's why everyone's in them), so you
get to enjoy that, and (2) will give you a
very essential break from the go-go-go on
consumption every once in a while.

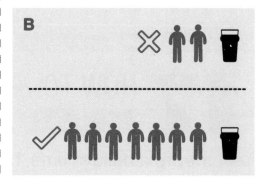

*That many people CAN be wrong, but they probably
aren't.*

FOR THE LOVE OF GOD, EAT SOMETHING.
And not just those hard pretzels people
wear around their necks at these things.
Smuggle in a sandwich or SOMETHING.
With all that beer, you need ballast.

This part's easy to forget. Don't.

48 HOW TO *POUR A PERFECT PINT OF GUINNESS*

That most distinctive of beers requires an equally distinctive pouring method.

Many will tell you that the best Guinness can only come from a tap, but you can also find Ireland's most iconic alcoholic export in bottles and cans—which is very helpful if you don't, you know, own a bar.

But the proper pouring technique is the basically same for all of them.

STEP 1: Grab yourself a clean, room-temp pint glass (refer to hack 83). PLEASE avoid the standard shaker variety that you'll see everywhere, and instead opt for a glass that curves and flares out as it goes up, or, if you're really doing it right, has one of those fun little bubbles that pop out about three quarters of the way up.

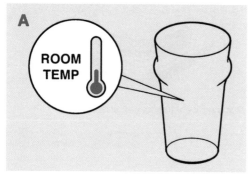

Cold = bad

STEP 2: Tilt your glass at a 45-degree angle, and begin pouring *niiiiice* and slowly until the glass becomes about three quarters full. Then stop. Not forever—there's more beer to come!

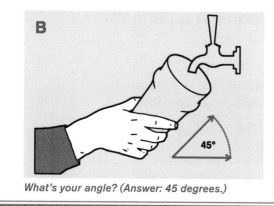

What's your angle? (Answer: 45 degrees.)

STEP 3: Good Guinness things come to those who wait. So do that. And then, wait some more. Stop considering drinking the beer right now. Drink another beer if you have to. Look into the cascading effect and ponder all the really smart, caring people who made you this beer. Just don't touch it! The "settle" is the quirkiest but also most important of a Guinness pour to get the proper flavor.

STEP 4: Once you can see a clear line between beer and creamy head, get back to pouring—this time, with the glass on the table at no angle. Keep filling until the head peeks *juuuuust* over the top of the glass, then stop.

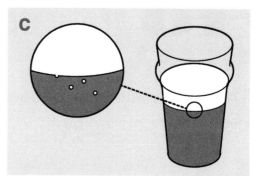

Toe the line.

STEP 5: Wait again. Seriously. I'm sorry. When everything settles once more, and you see that really clear beer-head border, you can cease being annoyed by me, and sip your perfect pint. You done good.

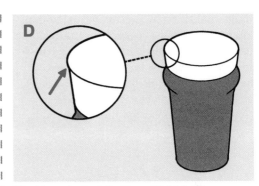

Would you look at that beautiful thing?

49 THE ONLY THING YOU REALLY NEED TO KNOW TO
SAFELY TAP A KEG

Or, how to avoid saturating yourself with beer right before everyone comes over

The twisting and clamping is cake. The crucial part: If the tap has a lever that locks said tap onto the keg, and that lever moves up and down . . . make sure it's up before you do anything else. The lever safely locks the tap to the keg, but it also deploys the device that plunges down into the keg to extract the beer. I've seen many, many a keg purchaser destroy his/her pre-party mood (and shirt) by aggressively slamming a tap whose lever is down onto the keg, and having it explode literally everywhere in a wet, foamy display of pressurized beer's true power. So basically, if you don't end up needing a shower and to borrow a benevolent soul's button-down, you did it right!

CLOSE

Keg parties are no fun if the keg attacked you beforehand.

50 THREE TIMELESS OKTOBERFEST BEER-CONSUMPTION RULES

No, none of them involve mandated lederhosen.

RULE 1: Only, only, only drink beers out of 1-liter steins.

RULE 2: Hoist those steins to cheers—although instead you'll ebulliently say "Prost!"—often and aggressively. The steins will not break, as they are designed for exactly such jovial work.

RULE 3: Realize that Oktoberfest actually begins in September.

PROST!

The Bavarian spirit is a good spirit.

51 ALWAYS, ALWAYS, ALWAYS *CALL THE FOAM "HEAD"*

Terminology is important.

Because . . . that's what it's called. If you really wanted to, you could also say "collar," but that makes your beer sound like a dress shirt, which is obviously no fun.

But not all beer head is the same. Some bubbles are large while others are quite fine; some beer types aren't truly themselves without a head almost the height of the beer itself, while higher ABV beers often pour with nothing more than a thin smattering of quickly dissipating foam. And some places take their beer head more seriously than others. In Belgium, long considered to be the epicenter of great beer before the craft movement really took off in the US, much of the glassware is designed to ensure the right-size head for specific beers.

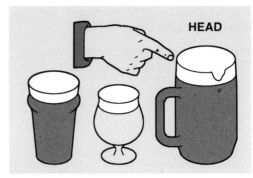

HEAD

It's always head.

52 IT'S FUN TO CALL KEGS BARRELS, BUT ACTUALLY, CALL THEM "HALF-BARRELS"

If you're going to use technical terms, you may as well be correct.

A "barrel" is a roundish wooden container that beer used to be stored and shipped in, but it's also a unit of measure: In the UK, it means 43 gallons, in the US, 31 gallons. The standard-size frat-party keg, or barrel, that you see competitors in the World's Strongest Man toss over a bar, and that you have successfully tapped thanks to hack 49, is actually 15.5 gallons, or, yes: a half-barrel.

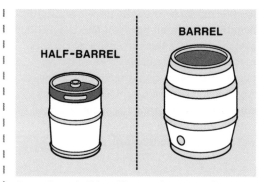

HALF-BARREL

BARREL

Sometimes half is still more than enough.

53 IN THE EVENT OF A NUCLEAR HOLOCAUST, *IT'S STILL OKAY TO DRINK THE BEER*

Maybe not the most fun thing to consider, but definitely good to know!

Ever thoughtful of people's true needs, in 1957, the US government ran a number of very important tests to see how nuclear blasts would affect packaged beverages. Their findings? Beer bottles and cans placed in close proximity to a nuclear explosion (1) largely survived intact, and (2) the beer inside was "well within the permissible limits for emergency use." So, long term, the beer might have a sliiiiight negative impact on how you feel (Might! It also might not!), but the entire world was just wiped out by nuclear war, so it's all about short-term survival for now anyway. And beyond the obvious need for a drink when that whole thing happens, the beer was recommended as a safe and usable water source. File that info away!

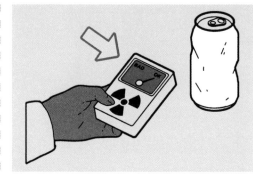

Enjoy!

54 NOBODY CALLS *BEER FROM SMALL BREWERIES "MICROBREWS"* ANYMORE

You shouldn't either.

So, microbreweries themselves are still technically a thing—the rule in the United States is that they need to create fewer than 15,000 barrels of beer a year to qualify as such. Hell, there are even "nanobreweries," which generally do very little output and are sometimes run by just a single person. But the product itself? Colloquially, it's all "craft beer" now! Has been for a while, actually. The old name never really made any sense anyway, unless the beers were served in a cup from a child's tea set. Which isn't enough beer.

MICROBREW

Other things it's not called: "tinysuds," "punylager," "really small beer."

55 GETTING *DEEP INTO YOUR LOCAL BREWERIES* IS VERY WORTH IT

Supporting your community is the simplest way to ensure you can continue to score fantastic beer.

You don't need to abandon that Vermont or Colorado or California beer you love so much, but local breweries are everywhere, and you should care about them. Especially when they're small. Support from smart, attractive beer lovers like yourself is exactly what keeps them going, and that community camaraderie is just cool and really irreplaceable. And since your local breweries aren't hamstrung by the concerns that stem from dealing with long-range distribution and delivering a consistent product all over the country, they are also doing the most innovative stuff with their beers and may have interesting releases all the time. Plus, any men working there probably have unfathomable beards, and they're all just nice people.

The first step is to find one, of course, which you can do by Googling around, checking out beer hashtags on Instagram, or . . . asking people who like beer. The second, hopefully none more daunting step, is to go say hi, and help keep them in business by drinking their delicious beer. And tip!

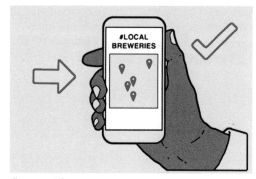

#supportthecause

56 WHILE THEY DON'T ALWAYS MAKE SENSE, *TAKE ADVANTAGE OF GROWLERS WHEN YOU CAN*

Save money while drinking fresh beer.

Growlers are vessels that let you tote around a whole bunch of beer and seal it up all tight so it doesn't lose carbonation or flavor. The classic versions are made from glass in 64-ounce and 32-ounce sizes, but intrepid companies have also created stainless steel and even copper growlers with intense pressurization systems to ensure your beer definitely stays fresh. You can get those from various websites, and most breweries or beer stores that fill growlers will sell you one of the glass variety.

Yes, growlers are more work in that you need to lug around a bulky container, but (1) they are often significantly cheaper to fill than buying bottles or cans, and (2) they basically force you to drink the beer within a day or two if you want it at its freshest and most carbonated. And any excuse for "just one more beer" is a strong one.

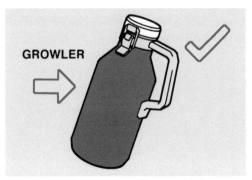

GROWLER

Always remember to close the cap tightly.

57 BREWERY TOURS *OFTEN MEAN FREE BEER*

Educate yourself while tasting the wares.

Yes, it's great to get walked through a brewery by someone who's devoted their life to making you a beverage you love, and get all the equipment and process explained. Knowledge! But often, at the end they'll reward your interest with a tasting flight of their wares—to, um, complete that education. Pick a brewery or two, and check their website or give them a call to see if they offer this. And even if they don't, beers poured on premises at breweries often tend to be nice and cheap.

FREE BEER

It's not a trick.

58 DRINKING BEER AFTER A WORKOUT IS *MAYBE, POSSIBLY BETTER THAN WATER*

Unless, of course, you overdo it.

Beer has electrolytes, replenishing sugars your body needs, and some doctors believe the carbonation helps quench the thirst that hits you after doing all that sweating. Plus, it'll make you, y'know, feel pretty good. And if this sounds like less of an occasional thing and more of a noble lifestyle you want to pursue more whole-heartedly, look to see if there's a local Hash House Harriers group in your area—they're crews of devoted runners who also often make a point of strategically stopping by bars on their route for a pint or two. Good people, them.

Sports!

59 KNOW WHAT TO EXPECT FROM CASK BEER BEFORE YOU ORDER ONE

A quick primer on a very distinctive and different type of beer

While the UK is where you'll find this very ancient and revered form of beer at its most abundant, some craft beer bars will also have a cask or two on hand. Yes, it's great for feeling like you're in 1686 (a noble goal indeed), but it's also . . . different. Cask beer—drawn out of the cask by a really cool hand pump with an even cooler name (beer engine) isn't carbonated and therefore lacks that familiar bubbly snap, which is the most immediately obvious difference. It's also generally served at a warmer temperature than you may be accustomed to. But it's absolutely worth trying one, to see if that's something you'd LIKE to become accustomed to.

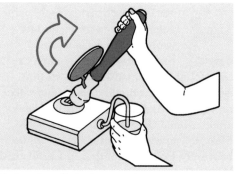

This here's called a beer engine.

60 PLAY THE BEST DRINKING GAME EVER: THE BOOT GAME

And if you play it smartly, all the beer will be free.

'm honestly not sure if this is a revered German tradition that's centuries old or my friends in college made it up. Either way, it's fantastic. Here's how it works:

FIND A BAR that will serve you beer in a two-liter glass boot. A literal boot, made of glass. They're amazing.

THE FIRST PERSON picks up that boot and drinks as much or little as they want. They then flick the boot with their finger to make a slight ringing sound, and pass it to the next person at the table. THE BOOT CANNOT TOUCH THE TABLE. If it touches the table, whoever is responsible for such an abominable action loses the game and has to pay for the entire boot. The next person does the same, drinking as much or little as they want and flicking and passing

and no-tabling, and so on, around and around the table.

Leave either as a champion who got free beer or a penniless disgrace.

HERE'S WHERE IT gets interesting. As this goes on, the boot will obviously begin to empty. The person who finishes the beer in the boot? They're fine. The person

BEFORE that person? They're the one who's in trouble: They lose and therefore have to pay for the boot. Which presents the dilemma as the beer level starts to get down there: Do you take a little sip, so as not to put the next person in a position to finish it, rendering you the loser/payer? Or do you just go for it, hoping upon hope that you can finish it off and not leave just a bit, making it simple for the next person to close it out? Big, big choices that seem easier to make as the night wears on, but obviously, that's just the beer talking.

GET ANOTHER BOOT and do it again.

A strategic master, clearly

Never forget the flick.

61 WANT TO BE EVEN *MORE LITERALLY SURROUNDED BY BEER THAN USUAL?* GO TO AUSTRIA.

For the times when a Jacuzzi full of boring old water just won't do it

Specifically, Starkenberger Brewery, which has, essentially, hot tubs full of 40,000 gallons of heated beer that you can take a dip in while drinking a much colder brew. Does it actually heal wounds and improve your skin, as they claim? Sure, why not!

If you for some reason still have a travel agent, call them immediately.

62 YOU CAN IGNORE *"BEER BEFORE LIQUOR, NEVER SICKER; LIQUOR BEFORE BEER, YOU'RE IN THE CLEAR"*

No cheeky rhyme can limit you any longer!

There's no scientific evidence to back it up. And, in fact, if you drink a whole bunch of liquor early in the night and don't keep it in check before switching to beer, you'll be anything but in the clear. However, one of beer's better self-regulating qualities is it makes you feel full. Which, ultimately, means you can drink beer whenever you want, kind of, in some ways!

IGNORE RULES

FREEDOM!!!!

63 WANT A *BEER WITH YOUR BIG MAC AT MCDONALD'S?* YOU CAN DO THAT.

Sadly, the refills are not free.

I n the comfort of an actual McDonald's in France, Greece, Portugal, Germany, South Korea, or Austria, you can order a pint to go with your Value Meal. Other fast food places also offer the same very wonderful level of service.

YES

YES

European innovation at its finest

64 THE ONE TRUE TECHNIQUE FOR *SHOTGUNNING* A BEER

How to mitigate spillage, injury, and embarrassment

Yes, it's borderline dangerous. And also largely for people who apparently hate the taste of beer and just need to GET IT DONE. But shotgunning a can of beer—the process of rupturing a hole in the aluminum, cracking open the top, then coming to the proudly stunned realization that you just consumed an entire beer in 3 seconds—is an activity that can be quite exhilarating, if also juvenile, and potentially requiring a trip to the dry cleaner. Although the last one can be avoided if you follow these simple steps.

STEP 1: Grab your can. Twelve ounces is standard, but advanced shotgunners have been known to do the deed with 24-ounce beers or even larger. Proceed with caution if you choose to make such a size upgrade—those people are crazy, yes, but also crazily well practiced—and hold it parallel to the ground, with the tab pointing down and the drinking-hole (the official name) pointing up.

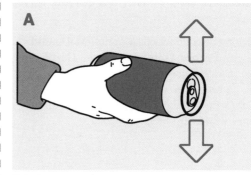

Tab down, opening up

STEP 2: Grab a key with a pointy end or a knife whose pristine edge you really don't give a crap about, and jam it into the top side of the can AWAY from the drinking-hole end, about a half inch from the bottom. Work your slicing device around to cut a small, square hole about ¾" × ¾", being very careful to (1) not cut yourself on it or the can itself, (2) not leave any jagged edges facing outward, and (3) not spill any beer, as that would be cheating. The hole size is crucial here: "No garage doors" is a key phrase to keep in mind.

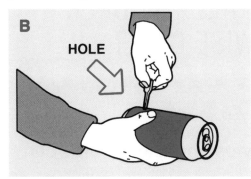

No garage doors!

STEP 3: Hold the beer steady, with the hole you just cut facing upward to prevent spills. Loudly execute a theatrical countdown, then crack the tab and immediately hurl your head backward so your mouth is facing the sky, and plant the freshly cut hole directly onto your mouth.

STEP 4: Tilt the can at more and more of an upward angle as the seconds tick by, so all the beer rushes into your mouth, gulping desperately as you go.

Smooth motion = success

STEP 5: When the can is empty and all the beer is inside you, breathe once more, then turn the can upside down so you can prove that there is no beer left and that you are a champion. If there IS beer left, allow your friends to call you literally whatever mean names they want. You deserve it.

Just trying hard doesn't count for anything.

STEP 6: Graduate college.

65 HOW TO GET ALL THE BEER YOU OTHERWISE CAN'T:

THE WONDERFUL WORLD OF BEER TRADING

Yes, you've got to put in some work, but the rewards can be endless.

Some of the best beers out there are only sold super locally, or are made in extremely limited quantities, or are otherwise unavailable to you. Luckily, they all can be yours with a little effort, and everything's more rewarding if it makes you put in a bit of work. Except for actual work, of course.

The beer-trading landscape is a wide and often crazy one, and if you get into it you'll unlock enough ideas for an entire book called *Beer Trading Hacks*, which I will buy. But here's the super-brief primer:

FIND A PERSON who lives in an area heavy with fantastic and unique beers, who also loves the stuff and wants similarly rare beers in return. Most people start with a friend, or a friend of a friend, but you can also seek out potential trading partners in beer-crazed message boards on sites like BeerAdvocate.com. Googling will get you places.

A

CRAZY 4 BEER MESSAGE BOARD

Find your people.

FIGURE OUT WHICH beers people want that are only available near you. In trading, beer is currency—the only one. So you need something amazing that someone somewhere else can't get their hands on.

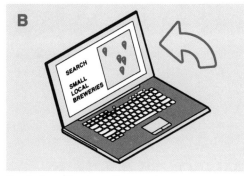

B

Track down the beer they want.

LEARN THE LINGO. There are far too many slang terms for specific beers and breweries to list here; if you get in deep, you'll need to Google those too so you don't raise red flags as some sort of beer-thieving charlatan. But here are two you definitely need for starters: "ISO" = "in search of" (the beers you want), "FT" = "for trade" (the beers you have)."

TELL POTENTIAL PARTNERS what you can send them and what you yourself are looking for. Then buy what they want. You are now a solitary Federal Beer Reserve.

DO NOT DRINK the beer. That makes it much less appealing to potential trading partners.

PACKAGE, PACKAGE, PACKAGE! Beer is also less appealing when it's been soaked into cardboard after its bottle breaks during shipping. There are all sorts of beer-specific sleeves and other materials you can buy, but tons of bubble wrap and ensuring the box is tight and nothing's moving around will generally do the trick. You'll also want to put each individual bottle in a large Ziploc bag—if something goes wrong, you don't want everything to be sticky and disappointing, too.

SHIP THEIR BEER, and wait for yours to come. It's much more fun than checking the mail in hopes of *Coldwater Creek* catalogs.

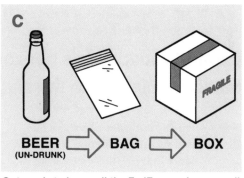

C

BEER ⇨ **BAG** ⇨ **BOX**
(UN-DRUNK)

Get ready to know all the FedEx people very well.

PLAY THE GAME right. Don't scam people. Deliver on what you promise. Throw in an extra less-rare beer or two for free, to make people love you. Stick with the outlook that most beer traders have: Beer should be traded for beer and never for money.

DRINK! THIS IS very similar to standard drinking of untraded beers. If you need to Google how to do this, you're probably in need of a different hobby.

Your pen pal never set you up this well.

66 THE BEST WAY TO *TASTE A WHOLE LOT OF BEERS, ON THE CHEAP*

Expand your palate's horizons while spending time with friends aiming to do the same.

Figuring out what beers you like and sticking to them is a noble move indeed—there's nothing more defeating than seeking out something new, coming home all excited, then taking one sip and having to execute a drain pour. THE PAIN!! But . . . your next true beer love may very well be out there, just waiting for you to embrace it (with your hand) and tell it how much you want to be with it forever (then swiftly drinking it).

So what does a conflicted beer drinker do? Host a tasting party, a wondrous event that provides a shortcut in both time and expense to expanding your beer consumption horizons.

WHAT YOU'LL NEED:

Friends who love beer

Failing that, people you DON'T like, but who like beer, and who you can tolerate if you've had a couple of those beers

A directive to everyone to bring two or three bottles or cans of their favorite beers

Some small glassware

Probably some chips

The execution is simple: Line up the glasses, open the first beer, and give everyone an equal amount. Then repeat, repeat, repeat. Bombers are best so everyone can get a little more, but as long as the gang can agree to not be greedy, small pours from a twelve-ounce can or bottle shouldn't matter—this is all about trying a bunch of things to figure out what you dig. Also, taking notes is definitely a good idea. You're not going to want to! But you really should. You'll see.

People will come. People will most definitely come.

67 AND WHEN THE PARTY'S WINDING DOWN: *MAKE A CUVÉE OF ALL THE BEERS*

It's like Jungle Juice, but . . . with beer.

Cuvée is a French wine term that literally translates to "tank" or "vat" but is often used to describe a blend of various different wines. For beer, that's exactly what it is, too. If you can be judicious enough to save a bit of every beer you drink at your tasting, you can put them all together at the end to create something unique and unholy and beautiful.

Okay—potentially beautiful. It's completely possible given the combo you use that the mix comes out horrible! But the practice isn't as ludicrous as it sounds— many brewers create special bottles that blend all their favorite products into one and release them only once a year, and people go bonkers for them. Of course, they try dozens of mixtures to nail it and, you know, do this for a living. But that doesn't mean you shouldn't take a shot, too.

IMPORTANT NOTE: Cuvée creation works best when similar-ish beer types are blended—it can sometimes be difficult to get, say, a barleywine and a triple IPA to hold hands and really love each other.

Maybe get just slightly more scientific than this.

Fun DIY Projects
Employing Beer Bottles

R ecycling is a swell thing to do, but it also means your empty beer bottles end up sad and lonely, and beer bottles deserve better than that. One way to solve that problem? Transforming them into all sorts of handcrafted items you'll end up using all the time. But unlike at summer camps when you were seven, you get to light things on fire to make it happen!

68 TURN YOUR *BEER BOTTLES INTO DRINKING GLASSES* (FOR BEER, OF COURSE)

Now we're getting serious: You're about to light stuff on fire.

WHAT YOU'LL NEED: One beer bottle of your choosing (make it good and handsome!), a dish full of acetone (or most nail polish removers will do), a rag or paper towel, a nicely sized length of cotton string or cooking twine, a lighter or matches, coarse- and fine-grit sandpaper, oven mitts, a bowl with water and a bunch of ice, and a willingness to, again, light things on fire

STEP 1: Drink your beer. This is very important. Skipping this step will make this project impossible and make you, personally, far less happy.

If you don't drink your beer, you can't make cool stuff.

STEP 2: Scrape the label off as best you can, then dab a rag or paper towel into the acetone and scrub it against the remaining flecks of label; they should come right off.

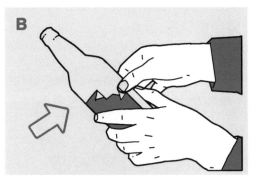

Label removal is annoying but worth it.

STEP 3: Fill that large bowl with water and plenty of ice. You're going to use this as a safety measure and also at the end of the process.

STEP 4: To create your glass, you're going to be heating up the bottle enough to break at a point of your choosing. Things to consider: how tall of a glass you want, and (likely) ensuring you don't torch through a part of the embossed logo that you want to look at. Take your yarn, figure out where you want that cutoff line to be, and wrap it around the bottle four or five times with enough yarn left over to tie it tight—but don't make that knot just yet.

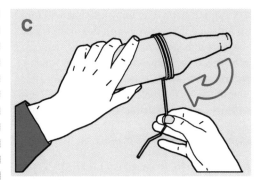

Measure it out.

STEP 5: Pour some of the acetone into a dish or bowl, and drop your now-measured length of yarn into it for as long as it takes to seem totally saturated. Then take it out and wrap it back around the bottle at your desired spot in a level fashion, and tie it tight. Check to see if your nail polish is still there.

Acetone bath!

STEP 6: It's here! The fun part that will make up for your manicure being destroyed. Bust out your lighter or matches and set that yarn majestically ablaze, slip on the oven mitts, and rotate the bottle at a medium pace for a count of 40 to 50 seconds. Do this over the ice bath you created earlier—if anything starts to go crazy flame-wise, just bail and drop the bottle in.

Be careful, please.

STEP 7: When the count is up, drop the bottle in the ice bath, and—MAGIC IS REAL!—it should immediately separate into either two or three pieces: the third potentially being a smaller middle section the string is wrapped around, with the top (neck) and bottom sections separating themselves as well. If the bottle doesn't come apart on the first shot, it's possible you might need to get another run of yarn and light that one up, too, depending on the bottle, but that's all right—you're still an okay person.

Magic: real once more.

STEP 8: Pull the almost-there glassware out and let it sit for at least 10 minutes, then take your sandpaper to the newly burned edge and make it as smooth as possible, working from coarse grit down to fine. If you want to step it up (or just have somewhere to be soon) you can get a diamond-coated sanding disk for any power sander you may have. But all of this is very important—even the coolest beer bottle glass won't make up for a wildly lacerated mouth.

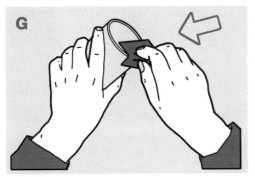

G

Don't skimp on the sanding.

STEP 9: Rinse it, then—Drink! Beer!

NOTE: Getting the bottle to split on a nice clean line largely involves really detailed string placement, which will probably take some (fun) practice. You can also purchase a glass bottle cutter from any crafts retailer, which cuts very accurately! But which also means nothing gets lit on fire.

69 WHEN YOU MAKE ENOUGH GLASSES, *KEEP GOING AND MAKE SOME CANDLEHOLDERS*

Deploy the techniques you learned in hack 68 to create some mood lighting.

t's basically the same process as the glasses project before this one, except you may want to cut the bottle a bit shorter (but not at the expense of beheading the St. Pauli Girl or anything), and tea candles, which, unfortunately, are not beer, will go in at the end. If you want to get really ambitious, you can melt down

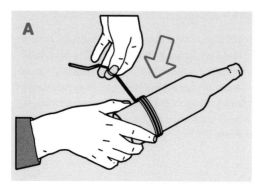

String it low and get ready to light it up.

a fancier candle from a silly, non-beer-bottle jar and have it drip into your creation, then replace the wick before it hardens.

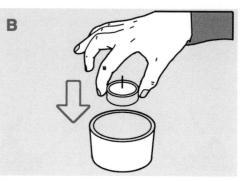

More fire

70 AND DON'T THROW OUT THE NECKS—*USE THEM TO MAKE SHOT GLASSES*

Let no part of the beer bottle go to waste.

Since you likely burned through your bottle fairly well below the start of the neck while making the glass or candleholder, you'll have to string it back up to properly create these guys, but that's okay—just be even more careful, since you won't have as much to grab onto that's far away from the flame. Remember that glass bottle cutter you were strongly encouraged not to get in hack 68, because fire is cool? Well, if you DID happen to get your hands on one, maybe as a birthday gift from someone who wanted you to make them shot glasses out of beer bottle necks, now might be a decent time to use it.

WHAT YOU'LL NEED: A bottle, string, acetone, ice, water, bottle caps, and some superglue

STEP 1: Make the ice bath. Measure out that string and get it soaked in acetone. Then wrap it around the bottom of the neck, tie it, and set it ablaze.

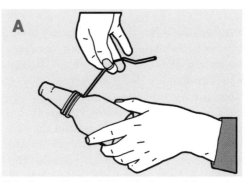

This time, string it right at the base of the neck.

STEP 2: Drop it in the ice bath, as in hack 68, and then take it out. After it's sat for a bit, do the same sanding that you read about in the glassware-from-a-beer-bottle section.

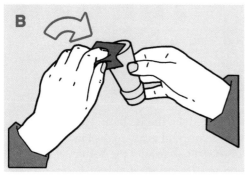

Sanding is key—your mouth is going here.

STEP 3: Take a bottle cap that hasn't been bent in half and instead just had its edges tugged up, add some superglue, and lightly dab it around the inside of the cap's ridges. Then press it into place on top of the bottle neck. Your best bet is to use a twist-off cap and work it into the grooves of the threading, then twist it on tight. If you use too much superglue, it'll leak out onto the bottom of the cap and might be tough to scrape off, so just be very judicious.

Screw it or glue it on.

STEP 4: Let it sit for a while and pour in some water to ensure you've got a tight seal. Then pour out the water and fill it with something even more fun.

Celebrate your abilities, with booze.

STEP 5: Remember that it's okay to drink things that aren't beer, as long they're coming out of a piece of glassware that you made, out of a bottle that once DID contain beer.

71 OR GUITAR SLIDES

Yes, this one's a little specific, but you can't JUST make shot glasses all day.

WHAT YOU'LL NEED: One of those necks you just acetone-flamed off (preferably from a more wine bottle–looking, large-format beer bottle), and that's kind of it.

STEP 1: Sand, sand, sand, unless you care not for your fingers' health/are able to quickly recover from extremely deep cuts because you are, in fact, Wolverine.

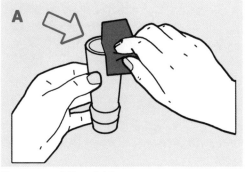

Saaaaaaand *the night away . . .*

STEP 2: Slide that sucker onto your finger and play the *bluuuuuues*. Or just pretend like you are, while holding a guitar and playing the bluuuuuues on Spotify.

Nothing says rock 'n' roll like a crewneck sweater.

72 MORPH YOUR *BOTTLES* INTO *TIKI TORCHES*

Perfect for repelling bugs as you create more empty bottles for future crafts

Drinking beer outside is why the earth invented summer, but, unfortunately, it also invented mosquitos, who love you even more when you drink beer, as you learned in hack 35. And while there are a million ways to deflect the little bastards, using old beer bottles and about 7 minutes of your life to ward them off seems beyond appropriate.

WHAT YOU'LL NEED: An empty, washed-and-dried beer bottle with the cap (make sure it's not severely bent in half); a premade wick you can find at a hardware store or, failing that, a length of not-super-thick-but-also-not-thin cotton rope; a Phillips-head screwdriver; a hammer; a piece of wood you have zero feelings about; citronella oil; maybe some pliers

STEP 1: Take your bottle cap and place it on the wood, ready the screwdriver to be hammered directly through the middle of the cap, then pound away. You want the hole to (1) exist, and (2) be large enough that your rope will *juuuuust* slide through but won't fall back out.

A

CAP

A couple of good whacks should do it.

STEP 2: Run that rope through the hole.

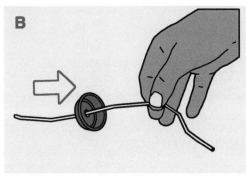

It's in the hole!

STEP 3: Fill the bottle up with citronella oil, maybe three quarters of the way up.

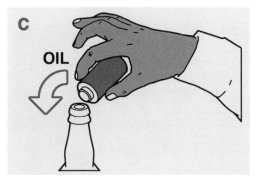

Anti-mosquito juice

STEP 4: Gently ease the rope into the bottle (GENTLY!!) until the cap is back where it started; if you're lucky you can just give it

a pop and it'll latch back on, but you might have to work it a bit with those pliers.

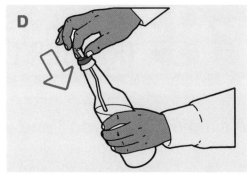

Make sure the rope goes well into the oil.

STEP 5: After waiting 15 minutes or so to allow the oil to be absorbed by the wick/rope, light it and let it *burnnnnnnnnnnn*, and laugh at all the mosquitos who are normally dying to drink your beer-filled blood but have suddenly lost all interest.

Light it up.

73 MAKE SOME (RATHER LARGE) SALT AND PEPPER SHAKERS

A simple project you'll end up using every day

While salt and pepper are the life of any meal, the shakers that contain them often excel at being boring. Luckily, it's about a 2-minute process to craft some DIY shakers that will do their damndest to remind you to drink beer at every meal.

WHAT YOU'LL NEED: Two washed, dried, and emptied beer bottles, preferably clear or at least somewhat see-through (although that's not totally necessary); two screw-on bottle caps from a water or soda bottle; a drill with a very fine bit (or something that you know is good at collaborating with you to punch holes in things); salt; pepper

STEP 1: Drill five or so *preeeeeetty* small holes in the top of the bottle caps, or grab your hole-punching tool and push it, push it real good.

Oooh baby, baby.

STEP 2: Fill the bottles up—one with salt and one with pepper.

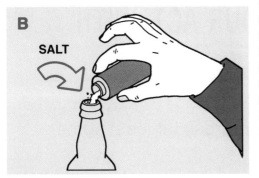

SALT

Just dump it in there.

STEP 3: Slap that cap on tight and make sure nothing's hurtling out the sides.

STEP 4: Make sure not to spill the salt. Except on your steak, over and over.

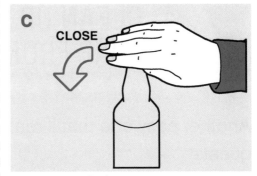

CLOSE

'Tis the season(ing).

BONUS HACK! These shakers can also be the perfect receptacle to store and distribute your top-secret blend of meat seasonings for grilling that everyone raves about. Even if those seasonings are . . . just salt and pepper.

74 CLEAN UP YOUR ACT, WITH SOAP FROM *A BEER BOTTLE DISPENSER*

Another easy one that'll really impress (at least some) guests

There's a less simple way to do this that involves getting actual soap pumps and fastening them to your bottle, but since your time has been completely consumed by reading this book, here's the quick way to get your hands clean without getting them too dirty first.

WHAT YOU'LL NEED: One clean beer bottle, one liquor pourer spout (one of those little metal things on the top of booze bottles in a bar), soap

STEP 1: Fill the bottle with soap.

This hack is just good clean fun [facepalm].

STEP 2: Jam the liquor pourer spout into the bottle.

Don't accidentally leave this one on your bar cart.

STEP 3: Wash your hands of any more labor, because that is IT, my friend.

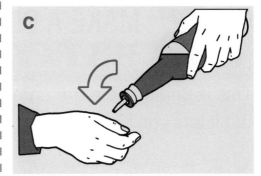

Take that, Dial!!

75 MAKE A PLANTER *THAT WATERS ITSELF*

This is one of the more complicated hacks in the book, but it lets you turn science into laziness.

You may (rightly) consider beer to be more important than water, but silly plants tend to disagree sometimes. Luckily, you can create a tidy little home for your houseplant that allows it to be ensconced in a cozy beer bottle while getting all the water it needs, with you doing absolutely nothing (after you do one small thing: make it).

WHAT YOU'LL NEED: One beer bottle (long necks are better for this particular project); one glass that's taller than the bottle's neck is long; one small piece of screen or other metal mesh; some string; acetone; a lighter; a big bowl of water and ice; oven mitts; some potting soil; a plant that you care deeply about (not a weird way to feel about a plant at all!); water

STEP 1: Go back and read about how you make drinking glasses from beer bottles in hack 68.

Yes, there are other hacks in this book. Read them, too.

STEP 2: Light up that acetone-y string and burn through the bottle about an inch to two inches below the base of the neck. You will ultimately turn the remaining bottle upside down, so the best way to do this is to picture the bottle with the neck down and the top up. Measure and burn appropriately.

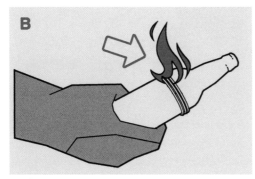

En fuego!

STEP 3: Take a second piece of string (not the one you just lit on fire), and tie a knot at the top. Then slice a tiny hole in the screen and place the string through it.

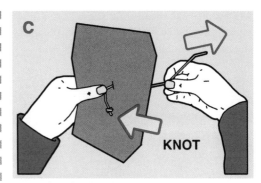

KNOT

Knot a bad hack right here.

STEP 4: Nudge the screen into place at the bottom of the neck of the bottle, ensuring the string falls down to the end of the part of the neck out of which you just sucked all the beer. Once this thing's placed into the glass, the water will climb the string through osmosis or something and reach the soil to keep it good and moist.

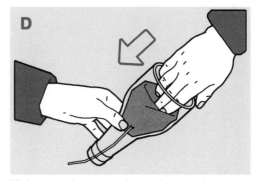

Make sure the screen is good and tight against the bottle's walls.

STEP 5: Fill the remaining piece of the now-neck-heavy bottle with potting soil (be sure the neck opening is pointing down) and your beloved plant of choice.

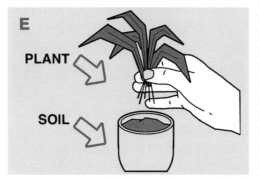

Something like a spider plant works better than, say, an oak tree.

STEP 6: Add water to the glass, then place the end of the bottle into the glass and never come back again. Okay, maybe check once a week and just keep it full.

Always give your plant free refills.

Everything You Need to Know About
Glassware, Serving Temps, and More

Zach Mack

Drinking beer from bottles and cans is in no way discouraged in this book, but sometimes, you want a beer AND simultaneously feel the need to prove to the world that you are capable of handling even more breakable objects, like glassware. But also, glassware has some real advantages, most notably that it helps the beer "open up," so it can better reach its true flavor potential.

Theoretically, you can drink any beer out of any glass—or hell, even a coffee mug with "poop juice" printed oh so cleverly on the side. But certain beers live and taste best in certain glassware, and maximization of your enjoyment can get a little scientific at times.

Which is why we recruited Zach Mack, a certified Cicerone (basically a beer sommelier who passed many near-impossible exams that made him drink a ton), who also owns ABC Beer Co. in Manhattan's East Village, to lay out the specific particulars of choosing glassware properly.

Glassware

76 FOR BOLDER BELGIAN BEERS WITH SPICE AND AROMA, BUT ALSO FOR SOME AROMATIC IPAS, THE MOVE IS A . . .
CLASSIC BELGIAN TULIP

The bowl-shaped body allows for ample head (the cool name for foam, remember?) retention space, while the tapered opening traps all the wonderful dancing aromas and funnels them straight into your willing nose.

STYLES THEY'RE BEST FOR: Belgian IPAs, Belgian goldens, Belgian dubbels, Belgian tripels . . . (you get the point), saisons, dry-hopped IPAs, imperial/double IPAs

BELGIAN IPA

Classy without trying too hard

77 FOR CLASSIC ENGLISH STYLES AND MILD AMERICAN COUNTERPARTS WITH LOWER ABV, LOW- TO MEDIUM-HEAVY BODIES, AND GENERALLY MILD FLAVORS, TRY A . . .

NONIK PINT

Not to be confused with a traditional shaker glass, Noniks are defined by the bulging ring around the top third of the glass that makes them easier to stack without damaging.

STYLES THEY'RE BEST FOR: Irish dry stouts, porters, English pale ales, nut brown and English brown ales, Extra Special Bitters (ESB), American IPAs, American pale ales, pilsners, saisons, Berliner weisses, goses

IRISH DRY STOUT

If your Irish pub doesn't feature these, you may need a new Irish pub.

78 FOR WHEAT-BASED BEERS, YOU WANT A ... *HEFEWEIZEN GLASS (OR "VASE")*

The taller body and wider top helps accommodate the larger head these beers throw off, and also looks really tall and elegant, just like yourself after a few.

STYLES THEY'RE BEST FOR:
Hefeweizens, American wheat beers, dunkelweisses, weizenbocks

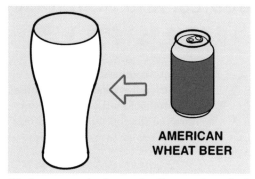

AMERICAN WHEAT BEER

Works as an actual vase, for flowers, in a pinch

79 FOR IMPACTFUL BEERS WITH DEEP FLAVORS, INTENSE AROMAS, AND HIGHER ABV, LOOK NO FURTHER THAN A . . .

BRANDY SNIFTER

The smaller size keeps your consumption in check with the higher alcohol "bigger" beers and also helps promote their often deeply fruity aromas right to the ol' nose.

STYLES THEY'RE BEST FOR:
Barleywines, imperial stouts, Scotch ales (or wee heavy), Belgian Strong Dark Ales, or most of those blessed brews that are barrel aged

SCOTCH ALE

The best way to enjoy the big dogs

80 FOR AN ORNAMENTAL HAPPY HOUR WHEN YOU'RE OPENING ONE OF YOUR RARE, RICH BELGIANS THAT YOU SCORED IN A BOTTLE SWAP, GET FANCY WITH A . . .

CHALICE OR GOBLET

While these have less of a technical aspect to them compared to other glassware, they're similar in shape to the vessels monks have used to enjoy the beers they've brewed for centuries—a few glasses will make you wonder how in the world they keep those vows of silence.

STYLES THEY'RE BEST FOR: Belgian Strong Dark Ales, dubbels, tripels, quadrupels . . . basically, all of those high-alcohol imported wonders

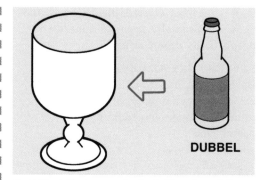

DUBBEL

Excellent if you are, in fact, the star of **Game of Thrones**

81

FOR EASY-DRINKING, LIGHT, OR EFFERVESCENT LAGERS, YOU WANT A . . .

PILSNER GLASS

This style was invented more to showcase the clarity and light color of the beer (kind of like a Champagne flute), but the glass itself feels nice in the hand and gives you a small stem to hold and keep you from heating up the liquid—which you do want to remain colder than, say, a Belgian dubbel—with your hand.

STYLES THEY'RE BEST FOR: German and Czech pilsners (duh), American adjunct lagers, kölsches, altbiers, dark and light lagers

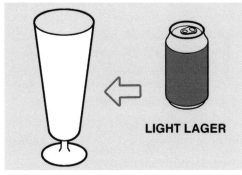

LIGHT LAGER

Fill this one to the brim.

82 AND, FOR USING IN A PINCH WHEN YOU MAY NOT HAVE A TULIP, CHALICE, OR SNIFTER HANDY, YOU CAN ALWAYS FALL BACK ON A . . . *LARGE RED WINE GLASS*

They help add that touch of class, while also being great at minimizing hand contact between your hand and the glass, slowing down the warming process.

STYLES THEY'RE BEST FOR: Mostly anything you would put in a tulip or snifter

MORE IMPORTANT NOTES ON GLASSWARE: There will be plenty of times where you may not have the exact right glassware for your beer, which is totally okay. Pouring your beer into any glass will lead to a better drinking experience than out of the can or bottle (as it helps release carbonation trapped in the liquid).

MINIMIZE HAND CONTACT

The jack of all glasses

83 NEVER USE *FROZEN GLASSWARE!*

Despite what your local sports bar might have you believe, you should never be freezing your glasses. First off, ice crystals cause beers to immediately foam over, leaving you with a lot of waste and an instantly flat beer. Second, the crystals will dilute the beer, which was intended to taste great just as it is, without being watered down. And finally, when those same ice crystals form, they absorb the odor and taste of the freezer they're in, and guess what: Nobody cleans their freezer. Including you. Besides, they make your beer too cold to actually taste.

Beware!

84 BUT IF YOU *ABSOLUTELY NEED A COLDER GLASS*

t's better to chill your glass bartender-style: by filling it with a few cubes of ice and some water for a minute or so, then dumping out and refilling with beer.

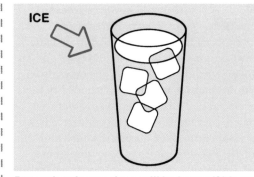

But seriously, your beer will be better if it's not freezing cold.

85 *RINSING YOUR GLASSES* IS KEY

O therwise, they'll be full of soap and oils, dust, and whatever the inside of your cabinet smells like. A quick 2-second dousing of tap water that completely rinses out the inside surface of the glass should be more than enough, and it'll help promote less foamy pours.

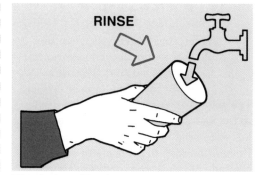

RINSE

Simple, but effective

86 STAY AWAY FROM *TRADITIONAL* SHAKER PINT GLASSES

Yes, they're everywhere in the beer world, but it's important to point out that they were never intended for beer service. The glasses themselves (which are used as the non-metal half of a cocktail shaker kit) were used by bartenders in a post-Prohibition rush to get beers to customers, a decade after all other dedicated beer glassware had been tossed out due to lack of use. Many of today's shaker pints are often even a deceptive ploy, using thick glass bottoms to cheat you out of a couple of ounces of beer. You don't want 'em!

THICK GLASS

Beware again!

Serving Temperatures

This is the part many people (especially Americans) have the hardest time wrapping their minds around: Beer can be (and often is) served too cold! And despite the terrible jokes about warm English beer, the difference of a few degrees can make a massive difference in flavor.

87 *35 TO 40 DEGREES*

Considered too cold for many beers, with the exception of mass-produced lagers from which you don't really angle to get much flavor. It's worth noting that anything poured near this temperature will rise to normal serving temperatures pretty quickly in a handheld glass. This is why those last few stomach-turning sips of warm adjunct lager always taste completely different than the first.

STYLES THEY'RE BEST FOR: Macro lagers, American adjunct lagers, light lagers

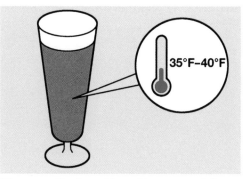

35°F–40°F

The worse the beer, the colder you want it.

88 *41 TO 50 DEGREES*

This is the desired range for most beers (both ales and lagers) to allow for full expression of flavor and aroma from the glass. Your safest bet? Taking that beer out of your home fridge 5 to 10 minutes before you want to drink it and letting it sit on the counter to get *juuuuust* right.

STYLES THEY'RE BEST FOR: Everything from IPAs to oatmeal stouts belong here. Stop drinking beer that's practically frozen! You will see!

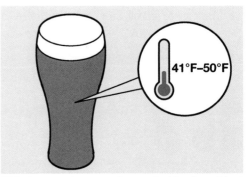

This is a sweet spot for probably the widest range of beers.

89 *51 TO 55 DEGREES* ("CELLAR TEMP")

Richer, higher-alcohol beers only really show their true, beautiful colors when they reach the serving temp that's barely cooler than red wine. Don't be scared: These beers should be consumed slowly and will naturally evolve in your glass as they warm up to room temperature, anyway.

STYLES THEY'RE BEST FOR: Rich Belgian beers like tripels and quadrupels, sturdy barleywines and wheatwines, heavy-hitting wee heavies (or Scotch ales), and dark lagers like doppelbock. Basically, if it veers toward wine strength in ABV, it's safe to assume it'll be at its best in this range.

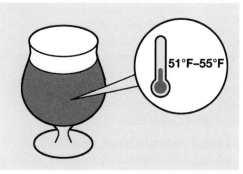

Don't be afraid to let bigger beers sit for a bit before you drink.

90 *55 TO 65 DEGREES*

English cask ales are usually hand pumped and served without refrigeration, which make for an altogether unique drinking experience that brings you close to drinking beer the way our ancestors might have. It may be different, but show some respect to your elders, dammit.

STYLES THEY'RE BEST FOR: English cask ales and certain cask versions of German kellerbiers are in their element at room temperature.

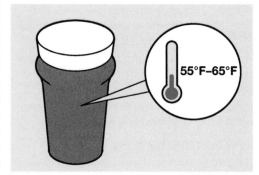

55°F–65°F

To be honest . . . beers at these temps are NOT for everyone.

But as is the case with ALL beverages, including Yoo-hoo, all of this is up to you. Trust your gut and play to personal preference, but don't be afraid to let a truly good beer sit for an extra minute or two before you get into it.

Storage Hacks

The four enemies of beer are light, heat, oxygen, and people who are just no fun at all. We're going to focus on the first three.

To be a good beer lover, keep your beer away from . . .

91 LIGHT

Why? Light breaks down the compounds in beer and changes the flavor. The term "skunked" actually comes from beer that's lightstruck, making it smell like skunk's spray. Clear bottles almost always end up skunked, and green bottles skunk almost as quickly. Only brown glass and opaque containers such as cans can stop beer from skunking.

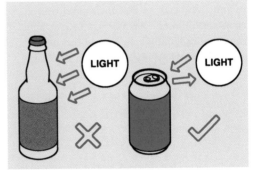

The evil must be stopped.

92 *HEAT*

Beer is a delicate food product, and fluctuations in temperature will cause said delicate compounds to break down, affecting the flavor in different ways depending on the style of beer.

Getting your beer hot even once will affect the flavor, so don't let it sit in the trunk of your car, near the heater or boiler in your house, or in an unair-conditioned room in summer. Consistency is key: Don't move beers from warm to cold (or vice versa) more than once, if you can help it.

Heat: Amazing movie, but terrible for your beer.

93 OXYGEN

Air exposure leads to oxidation, which over time makes your beer taste like cardboard or wet newspaper. So when you open it . . . drink it!

As much as you love O₂, your beer does not.

94 IF YOU HATE *SKUNKED BEER* . . .

Avoid buying anything packaged in clear or green bottles, or opt entirely for cans. If you're cellaring rare brews, find someplace dark to stash your bottles. Remember that fluorescent lights are just as bad as sunlight, so do make sure whatever storage place you choose can be kept dark 99 percent of the time.

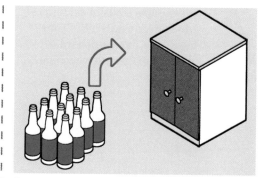

Dark = good

95 IF YOU'RE LOOKING TO *AGE YOUR BEER . . .*

Cellar temperatures are best for aging bottles, not unlike wine. Use your basement if you have one, or find a spot with the least fluctuation in heat, like an interior closet or dark garage.

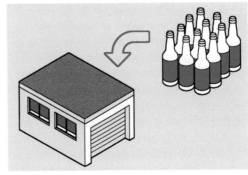

Let's grow old together.

96 IF YOU HATE *SPOILED, PAPERY BEER . . .*

Learn how to read bottle dates— which are either printed on the label, the side of the bottle, or most commonly, on the bottom, generally in MM/DD/YYYY format—and understand what you're drinking. Not all styles are cellar-worthy: Anything hoppy is intended for you to drink it as fresh as possible, and most beers with ABV below 7.5% won't hold up very well. Save the shelf space down there for your bourbon barrel–aged stouts, barleywines, and strong ales.

Bottle dates should be your bible.

How to
Infuse Your Beers
with New and Wonderful Flavors

B rewers spend their entire lives figuring out how to make your beer taste better, because they care about you. Specifically you! They're such great people. But many of those beers also provide a fantastic base to build upon by adding interesting flavors yourself. The most efficient approach is to use a French press, the coffee-making device that even Americans are now legally allowed to own.

97 THE *FRENCH PRESS*

Get ready to turn your kitchen into a mad flavor-scientist's lair.

For the uninitiated, a French press is a device generally used for brewing ground coffee. In its simplest form, it consists of an open-top cylindrical column and a cap with a plunger attached to a mesh filter. Normally, you put in the coffee grounds, let them steep with hot water, push the plunger down to strain, and pour. But we're going to unlock it for even more enjoyable use by swapping out the water for beer and the grounds for all sorts of wonderful, flavor-jammed ingredients.

Fun, but scary: The possibilities are endless here. You can infuse literally any ingredient into any beer, although most of those would be terrible ideas (see: Asparagus and Toothpaste Pale Ale). Read on for some fun recommendations for can't-miss infusions, but no matter what you add, the basic process is the same every time.

FRENCH PRESS

This simple little device can make beer magic happen.

- **ENSURE YOUR** French press isn't full of coffee. (Related: Why are you taking all that time to French press coffee and then aren't even drinking it?)

- **POUR IN** your beer—some French presses are only 12 ounces, which won't really allow you to put in a whole beer AND other ingredients, so hopefully you can find a larger one—then add whatever flavor enhancers you've decided upon.

- **PLACE THE** press in the fridge to let the flavors combine (called "steeping"; you'll learn for how long in hacks 98 and 99).

- **TAKE THE** press out, push down the plunger as far as it'll go, pour your fancy new liquid into a glass (all the added ingredients will remain in the press

thanks to the strainer), enjoy, and think about how to make adjustments to fit exactly what you're looking for next time. Significantly less toothpaste? Good call.

The joy of French press infusions is all in the creativity (and the beer drinking), so getting a little loose with what you play around with is the whole idea. But here are some recommendations to start you off as you get the moves down.

98 RASPBERRIES AND BLACKBERRIES IN A GOLDEN ALE

While this infusion won't end up tasting like fruit-forward sour beers you may have enjoyed, the berry kick is still absolutely distinctive—just dial it up or down to your preference.

Golden ales are ideal base beers for French pressing because they're fruity and fun without being hoppy, which means they generally won't conflict too much with other strong flavors. This particular infusion is perfect for hot summer days, unusually warm spring days, and bitterly cold winter days when, for whatever crazy reason, you want a golden ale that tastes like blackberries and raspberries.

YOU'LL NEED:

12 ounces golden ale (I used Russian River Damnation in mine, but plenty of breweries make great examples.)

1 ounce muddled blackberries

1 ounce muddled raspberries

Muddling is essential here: It'll release all the juices from the berries and allow them to mix with the beer. You can use an actual muddler (a thickish wooden stick bartenders use to unlock flavors by mashing ingredients, and also the most fun word to say in this entire book), or just mash up the fruit with the backside of a spoon in a bowl, then dump it all into the press. For this recipe, you'll want to steep in the fridge for about 15 minutes or so.

Don't forget to muddle!

The ratios here, as in all infusion recipes, are completely up to you, and something you should absolutely play around with. But I found this particular recipe offers delicious fruity flavor without overpowering the beer itself or turning it into something that would otherwise be found in a rectangular paper box that you stab with a tiny straw.

99 S'MORES STOUT WITH *GRAHAM CRACKERS, CHOCOLATE,* AND *MARSHMALLOW*

Does this sound ridiculously indulgent? Yes! But man, does it work.

Stouts are another fantastic beer bedrock for infusions, although for opposite reasons to the golden ale—they're SO thick and flavorful that they're difficult to overpower. Which ultimately means you can go pretty crazy.

I had some fun stout successes with about a half cup of toasted coconut (ALWAYS the unsweetened kind, never the sweetened) and vanilla bean (whose frightening price tag should really make us all appreciate that most basic of ice creams far more). But none of them allows a merry group of infused-beer drinkers to make deliciously terrible puns the way this s'mores stout will.

YOU'LL NEED:

12-ounce stout (If you really want to make it count, get something barrel-aged. They're expensive but always worth it—I employed a classic, Goose Island Bourbon County Stout. Although maybe start with something cheaper as you get your moves and preferred ratios down.)

One full-size (4.4-ounce) Hershey's milk chocolate bar (the kind you find on a convenience store rack), cut up into tiny pieces. (Yes, the whole thing!)

Two graham crackers, again, cut in tiny pieces

One marshmallow, also cut up

Pop everything into the press and put it into the fridge for about 25 minutes to steep. If you go with a standard stout instead of a barrel-aged variety, or one with less than, say, 9% alcohol, you'll probably want to cut that steep time or your beer may be manhandled (by the chocolate especially), but again, play around with it and find the balance that you enjoy. The ultimate result is about as beer-milkshake-y as one could ever hope for.

NOTE: Becoming tempted to spoon the mishmash of leftover infusion ingredients in the bottom of the press into your mouth does not make you deranged. Just, um, economical.

Campfire not required.

SECOND NOTE: Politely refrain from telling any hungry six-year-olds that you're doing this.

100

HOW TO *DO* *ALL THOSE* *AMAZING THINGS* WITHOUT *A FRENCH PRESS*

Chances are, you've probably got what you need just lying around your kitchen.

The foremost advantage a French press provides when infusing beer is the tidiness of it all—everything goes in, you wait, you plunge, you pour. But some of the benefits they provide while steeping coffee go away when doing even more fun beer stuff. Namely, that hot water unlocks the coffee grounds in a way that cold beer doesn't, and you're essentially just using it to strain out the added ingredients.

Which is great news, because it means that even if you don't have a French press, you can still infuse your heart out if you have a really finely woven mesh kitchen strainer.

FOR THIS HACK OF A HACK, YOU'LL JUST:

THROW THE BEER and infusion ingredients into a glass and place it into the fridge.

PULL THE GLASS out and pour through the strainer into ANOTHER glass.

DRINK THAT ONE.

Yes, you may spill some beer. Yes, you may scrape your tongue raw from uncontrollably licking remnant s'mores chocolate off the strainer. But you will still have deliciously hacked the hell out of your beer.

Strain, drink, enjoy.

Conclusion

Well, there it is. My only hope is that among all the learning and executing and hopefully not damaging too much of your personal property in the course of this book, you took the time to begin scheming up some of your own hacks. But most important, I hope you had a damn beer or two.

Acknowledgments

Thanks to my editor, Bruce Tracy; my agent, Stacey Glick; my publicist, Chloe Puton; Jean-Marc Troadec, Jessica Rozler, Suzie Bolotin, and everyone else at Workman Publishing; Sam O'Brien, who started me on this whole sudsy journey; ace illustrator Lee Woodgate; stud barman Nick Bennett; also-stud beer-bar owner and Cicerone Zach Mack (go find him at ABC Beer Co. in Manhattan); my beer fridge; my doctor; my dog, Frank, who sat under the desk licking my shins while I wrote this despite being very upset that I wasn't letting him outside to stare at squirrels; every single person who works at a craft brewery and does it for the love of the stuff; my brother-in-law, Scott; my father; and, of course, my mom, who makes this amazingly happy face whenever she takes a sip of a barrel-aged barleywine.

About the Author

BEN ROBINSON, the current editor in chief of *The Observer* and former chief creative officer of *Thrillist*, has written for *Deadspin, Huffington Post, Cigar World*, and numerous other websites and magazines, covering everything from the running of the bulls in Pamplona to a foolproof system for getting on *The Price Is Right*. He lives with his family, and his beer fridge, in Brooklyn, NY.